*For Kathleen*

To my parents Michael & Kathleen McMorrow
who instilled within me the gift of faith.
To my siblings who first taught me how to practice that faith!
To Eileen McMorrrow, an example of faithfulness.
To my son Michael who taught me
that I am capable of unconditional love.
To anyone involved in ministry of any kind.
To Sean MacDiarmada, 1883-1916,
the first writer and orator in the family tree.
And to working men and women everywhere.
May your lives be fruitful, free of struggle, and wildly prosperous!

# FOREWORD

Even before reading this book, I already knew Rev. Mike as an entertaining, affirming, intelligent preacher. I've known him as respectfully humorous, that he seems both confident and humble, that he exudes love, and that he presents himself as a person who wants always to grow.

I've known all of this from attending worship where he has pastored, while visiting my twin sister annually for a decade or so, and from his officiating at her memorial not so long ago.

I now appreciate Rev. Mike for his articulate expression of what "Religious Science" is. I think this little book could be an introductory text into Religious Science ("New Thought"). He cites theologians (Jesus, the Buddha....) and writes very well! He incorporates—often—his decades-long experience as a carpenter-contractor and his self-description as a "recovering redneck" (implicit in the title, *Blue Collar Spirituality*). Though men would benefit from his clear identification with maleness as a writer, women could easily benefit from reading it too (with a smile that THIS author is naming his maleness self-consciously—hence *thinking* of women readers).

McMorrow writes TO the reader, and expects OF the reader attention, and at least an attempt to implement the ideas he suggests. He wants the reader to live a joyous life that is fulfilling for him(her)self and those around the reader. The author includes exercises intended to foster action—along with his own experience of avoiding the very exercises he asks for!

I was born into "Religious Science." I realize in reading this book that I am still very much Religious Science to my core. Once the affirmation of life, available goodness for ALL, and an assumption of personal responsibility are ingrained, it's hard to get it out of one's system. I loved his humor combined with articulateness. I appreciated learning about carpentry and construction. I was glad he quoted from so many world religions, for they are all relevant. He's engaging, funny, and very honest. Any reader with a slightly embarrassing past could identify and feel accepted and affirmed.

One could not read this book without feeling or at least considering that "YOU MATTER."

This book may bring a person BACK TO or TO religion as s/he realizes that, as Rev. Mike writes, the goal is to "find a God that works." "There is a Power for Good in the Universe, and you can Use It!"

— Rev. Carolyn Jane Bohler, Rel.D., PhD. *God the What? What Our Metaphors for God Reveal about Our Beliefs in God*

# ACKNOWLEDGMENTS

There is a quality to those who have a connection to the land. Hearty and steadfast, solid and hardworking. In their youth, both of my parents had this experience in Ireland, which somehow transferred to the next generation, as my siblings all have a strong work ethic. I'll let others judge my own. To my cousins still at it in Currane and Kiltyclougher, you have my love and deepest respect.

I have to acknowledge the men I worked for over the years and who taught me the trade. Ed Croom, Dave Smuck, Nils Holm, Jim Guthrie of the Port Townsend days, whom I either worked for or learned the tricks of the trade from. John DeWitt, Rod Freeman & the rest of the Tunnel Rats from the House Doctor days. The California years: Doug Snyder, Phil Chauvet, Sandy Jackson, John Massey; all good guys and good bosses.

My customers from over 25 years of contracting in two states, thank you. To all of the men who worked for me through the lean years and some fat; we always stayed busy. I have to give a special shout-out to Dan Cirino. For 15-plus years we somehow survived each other! Thanks for the memories and the commitment to working hard.

My late business partner Gene Tummelo, the *keep sayin' that rosary* guy. We had a great run. Too bad we didn't get started earlier! I could write a book about any of these guys. All are great guys and real characters who were self-supporting, raised families, and raised a little hell in between.

I acknowledge the great teachers I've had along the way, and of course you always run the risk of leaving someone out. So, I'd better start with *the* Carpenter, whose teachings have kept me out of trouble when I followed them. Sista Judith Fogassy SDSH. Those who showed me the way to a New Thought: Ernest Holmes, Michael Beckwith, Eric Butterworth, Emmet Fox, Raymond Charles Barker, Dr. Sue Rubin, Rev. Dr. Moira Foxe at CSL Redondo Beach, Nancy Woods. And the ministers and practitioners of CSL Granada Hills, Dr. Jim Lockard and Rev. John MacLean—I miss our lunches! Dr. Kenn Gordon of

Kelowna, BC; long time teacher and first spiritual leader of Centers for Spiritual Living. You and Dr. Deb have shown us all how to live life in Principle and to have a great time doing it! Along with them, Dr. John and Barbara Waterhouse taught me the possibility of a marriage in ministry, and that it can be fun! Dr. Edward Viljeon, for demonstrating grace under fire, buoyed by a strong spiritual practice. You walk the talk, and I'm payin' attention!

It's taken me years to write this book. Years in construction, years of classes, years in ministry. It started when Christie Guymon made up a journal with "Blue Collar Spirituality" on the cover. Thank you for holding that vision for me. To my development editor Anita Rehker, for your guidance and enthusiastic support for the concept of the book. I could not have gotten this far without you. Big Love to you!

Dr. Jim Turrell of Newport Mesa, for your wisdom throughout the years and for getting me jumpstarted again on this project through your writers boot camp. It works! Here's the proof!

It's been said that life is what happens when you're busy making other plans. Marriage, Hawaii, Ireland; these were all highlights in a three-year layoff, until I read *The Assassination of Gabriel Champion* by our center's guest singer Angela Carole Brown. I'm so grateful you said *yes* to looking over what I had and for your support, enthusiasm, and light touch. You saw me through to the finish line—that's a feat in itself! Singer, Poet, Artist, Writer, Editor. A True Renaissance woman!

To my beloved teacher, Rev. Dr. Maureen Hoyt. You saw something in me all those years ago I had no clue was in there. You've been a teacher, mentor, ally, and friend; not to mention proofreader and grammarian! You've been a sister from the Cosmic Mister, to be sure! To say I love you doesn't cut it, but I do—and thank you for everything.

To my dearest Stephanie, my Love and partner in time. You show me every day the face of love and what partnership in love looks like. I love you and our life together. Onward and upward!

# CONTENTS

# For Anyone Who Works Outside

One cold January morning
On Discovery Bay, Frigid and Icy
Geese honking, stuck to the frozen pond
I consider revenge for yesterday's violation
By the Gander of Five
With drizzle softly falling
We scrape the ice
From the concrete slab.
Preparing for the chalk line snap
Laying out a room
For a life yet to be realized.
The winds blow now
Driving the drizzle turned sleet
Down the back of my...
Till now...warm, woolen, neck.
And still we scrape and snap
Clearing the deck
Of yesterday's scrap and waste
Making way for new walls waiting
To be nailed together
Stood in place—plumbed, lined and true.
Now with the North Wind
Bearing down harder still
We surrender to the Now
Sideways driven rain.
We pick up our rain-soaked tools
Roll up our cords
And take shelter in the truck—
Our refuge of warmth thawing
Our soaked-through jeans.

Reaching under the seat
We take a long pull on the
Flask saved for just this moment.
Cursing in our clothes—steam rising now—
Sodden with the tempest
Just unleashed upon us.
We start the truck
Heading for home
Turning from the gravel path
On to St George Road
Into the Brilliant Sunshine
Behind the Storm
As we realize we've just weathered
A Cold Front passing through
We look at each other
Beads of thawed water
Trickling off the end of our nose.
And I think to myself…
Next winter—California!


*Rev. M. McMorrow  8/13/10*

# Prologue

My name is Mike, and I am a recovering redneck!

I'm not making this claim as a badge of honor, but rather to acknowledge the man I once was, what happened, what it's like now, and how a science of mind guided me to a more inclusive way of being in the world.

Maybe it would be helpful to define what a redneck is and how you may be one without knowing it.

That great metaphysician Jeff Foxworthy has defined redneck for us to great laughter and at times a too close, too sobering, sense of reality.

In all honesty, my own neck is a lot more blue than red, but somehow a recovering Blue Neck just doesn't have the same ring to it.

As the past 5-7 years has been awfully concerning in this country, it turns out half of my ministry has been about speaking to difficult subjects on Sunday mornings. From Trayvon, to Ferguson (and astonishingly too many others), to #metoo, and to marriage equality before that. And I have to confess there's a part of me that has had certain opinions and a certain thinking about a lot of this, which is now in my past, but is a part of my journey. It has taken walking the spiritual path, THIS spiritual path, to discover, maybe even recover, my awakened nature.

And so, what I would like to say, here and now, in a public way, especially to women, is I hear you. I want you to know I now recognize how I and other working-class men of a certain un-woke mentality have been hurtful and how we have been wrong. To my LGBTQ brothers and sisters, many of us now understand, in a much deeper way, it is far more important THAT you love, than WHO you love. We know Black Lives Matter, and we are ready to step into being allies rather than complacent, even defensive, put-upon observers. And to reclaim that all beings are equal in the Light of Spirit, and Human Rights are Divine Rights.

Many men know this now. And it's imperative we sound our voices. And yet, we are still men. Which means we are not hairy women. And this means we can still be clueless and a bit thick.

Sometimes, like the Prodigal Son of old, we are going to stubbornly take things all the way to the pigsty before we are able to come to ourselves and see the world with new eyes.

And so, as we look around the world today, we're seeing the old conventions being trampled, and the race consciousness is in the very crucible of purification.

There is a new day longing to be set free. And what is being revealed is being revealed in order to be healed. One heart at a time. Even one redneck heart at a time.

Of course, when I first came to the study of the science of mind, or Religious Science, I didn't know there was a solution to my struggles. I really did think it was all my ex-wife's fault! I thought it was her, the economy, my employees, my business partner. And like many guys out there, I was angry and looking for somebody to pay.

At a certain point, I even returned to my religion of origin, following their BS rules, thinking that would protect my marriage and allow me to prosper. I focused on the idea of knowing God wouldn't give me more than I could handle. I believed my life of struggle was God-ordained. It was my duty to accept my burden with grace. God had a plan for me, and it was to offer my suffering up for the poor souls in Purgatory. I was wounded, aggrieved, and bankrupt in every area of my life. Yes indeed, folks, my life was a country & western, somebody-done-me-wrong kinda song!

I WAS that friend in LOW places.

Ernest Holmes calls this the morbidity of thought, and I had it in spades.

EH: *"Find me someone who is no longer sad, whose memory has been redeemed from morbidity, and I shall hear laughter."*

I have to tell you I wasn't laughing much when I got to Religious Science. But Religious Science is what taught me there is a Power for Good in the Universe available to everyone. Even me. And this changed my life.

It changed my life, and I know it can change the lives of working people everywhere. By the way, and in case you're wondering, the reason I keep speaking to working, blue collar people, and in fact, the reason for this book, is because that's what I came from. And I can tell you, ideas like the ones Ernest Holmes and Religious Science proffer are often seen by the working class as elitist, unavailable, and not relevant to our struggles. But that couldn't be more wrong.

Holmes came from the farm. He knew what it was to get his hands dirty. And he was inspired in ways I have not heard from anyone else, as far as speaking to working folk like me, to be something more.

But back to being a recovering redneck, which isn't to assert all blue collar folk are that, because we know that isn't so. I just know my story with having been all of the above. People are not born with red necks. You have to be taught. And I'll be frank; my University of Red-necked-ness came from 30 years in construction.

How I got into construction is kind of a mystery in itself, as I grew up in the middle of the Mojave Desert, on Edwards Air Force Base, which means I was surrounded by hundreds of miles of kitty litter. No construction guys anywhere. But I did take a few shop classes, which I loved, along with my college prep classes, which I slept through.

And I'd also been an Eagle Scout. It was there in the Sierras, where I regularly communed with some kind of magnificent presence beyond church, that I felt connected to something sacred. Except, I was not allowed to think of God or church in such ways.

I remember backpacking in Kings Canyon, and turning the corner, and the air got cooler, and there were yellow monkey flowers and red Indian paintbrush scattered all around. And suddenly there stood three majestic, giant sequoias. And in them, I saw Moses, Elijah, and Jesus. Standing there, thousands of years old, sentinels through time, with the God-rays breaking through the branches. I felt an unquenchable urge to genuflect, instinctively knowing I was in the presence of something godly.

It was my very first experience with feeling like I was standing on holy ground.

This started an odyssey of wanting to be a hippie, living in the woods, and at the same time hanging with the roughnecks in the forest industry. Eventually, this all led to construction. I learned the carpentry trade, and in time I could build damn near anything out of wood or concrete. As a contractor, I could study a set of plans and not only envision it built but I could put a number on it as well.

I learned how to work like a man, drink like a man, and fight like a man. It was a Neanderthal existence.

It was also a life of not thinking much beyond the next job.

And though some years were better than others, I could've gone the rest of my life waiting for the other shoe to drop. I'm no different from a lot of men, and now women, out there today, in that in spite of my skill level, I often spent as much time looking for work, as working.

And then when you do work, your wages are stuck right where they were five years before. And in your frustration, as the threat to your family grows, and the fear heightens, you look around for someone to blame.

The neck gets redder. The heart gets harder. And a guy with a hard heart can't hear much of anything but his own resentful thinking. As we all know, resentful thoughts sow the seeds of derision and strife. We're seeing that today.

So, this is where I was 20-something years ago. It's a place where many find themselves today.

I was at the start of a painful divorce. And not knowing what else to do with myself, I started reading a book by Emmet Fox I'd bought at a garage sale called *Sermon on the Mount*, inside of which, years before, someone had scrawled the words, "Science of Mind," and I thought, "Hmmm. Maybe they can do something about my thinking."

I read stuff like this from Ernest Holmes:

*"To suppose that the Creative Intelligence of the Universe would create man in bondage and leave him bound would be to dishonor the Creative Power which we call God.*

*"It is the inherent nature of man to express itself in terms of freedom.*

*"This is the simple teaching, the study of Life and the nature of the Law, governed and directed by thought; always conscious that we live in a spiritual Universe; that God is in, through, around, and for us."*

And Holmes started to blow my mind. I had never before thought of God as being FOR me. I was falling in love with a Power for Good, and I was learning to use it. My budding sense of Oneness was as yet undefined. I'd felt manipulated by religion, for sure, but I had no problems with Jesus. We were cool. After all, being carpenters, we were in the same union! In fact, we have a lot in common. He grew up in the desert; I grew up in the desert. He was a carpenter; I was a carpenter. He had 12 employees; I had 12 employees. He had long hair and a beard; I had long hair and a beard. He walked on water … I had long hair and a beard!

In all seriousness, I was being encouraged to broaden my idea of what the Living Spirit is. What Divine Intelligence means. What possibilities lay in an Infinite Field of Good, expressing as Love through Law. I wasn't sure what the hell that meant, and I didn't mind saying so. My new Religious Science community made it OK for me to be me. Rough edges and all. And they implored me to keep coming back. They saw the Truth FOR me, until I could see it for myself.

I can honestly call what happened to me during this time in my life a spiritual awakening. It's an awakening I've taken with me on my continued journey, and which I hope to share with you in these pages, to show anyone interested how they can experience such an awakening too.

Now, this book was not written to be placed under glass with the light of the heavens shining on it like a faded movie star. It is designed to be used! So, get your pencil handy—your hammer, nails, and drill for this time together—and be prepared to do a little work from the "tool box" I've provided at the end of each chapter. Even scribble notes in the margins, if you feel so compelled.

Are we ready? Then let's roll up our sleeves, and get to work!

# Chapter 1
# Struggle Is Not Set in Concrete

There is an aspect to life, which the working man experiences, talks little about, and often has no idea how to express. Simply put, he is so busy living a life full of struggle and mediocrity he just doesn't have the energy to take the time to sort through it all. Like materials left over from the job that just get stored away for "someday," he thinks about it tomorrow. In time, he is left with a yard full of clutter.

If this happens to be your life, this isn't a judgment but rather an observation of the life many people live. For self-employed folk, this is often complicated by the fact that "we eat what we kill," where if there is no sale, there is no money. Consequently, we move from job to job, rarely (if ever) taking stock of what we've learned as we chase down the next gig. And we never truly know for certain if our efforts have been profitable or not, until at last we visit the taxman at the end of the year. By that time, of course, it's too late.

If you can relate to this scenario, know you are not alone, and there is a way out.

There is a power already available to you that will point the way to success and profitability in every area of your life.

Through the next few chapters, we're going to explore what this power is and discover the many manifestations it takes. We're going to look at how to spot this power, how to cultivate it, how to use it to create the life YOU want to live. When you understand your life is not set in concrete, and your past need not keep you bound to an experience of struggle, pain, or futility, you will find yourself on the path to building your best life now, one step, one day, at a time.

## Pain Is Fated, Suffering Is Optional

Is it not self-evident that pain is a part of life? In any human life, even one that is most blessed, there is going to be disappointment, frustration, heartbreak, and grief through which we must all navigate. The ancient Hebrews observed long ago: *"to everything there is a season."* Pain is a part of life. For that matter, death is a part of life. But though pain is inevitable, suffering is optional.

Now, what do I mean by suffering? It's the belief system we heap upon any real hurt, and it IS self-inflicted.

Let's consider a hypothetical. One of the guys on your crew makes an error and you fly off in a rage, angrily thrashing around at anything and everyone. If this reaction is all you know, then, in that moment, and without tools with which to respond better and more instinctively, it's nearly impossible to stop and do it differently. But there ARE tools—tools this book will offer, tools that can help you access the power earlier mentioned. How big a deal is this, really? Well, if your outburst cost you the contract, then I'd say it was a pretty huge deal, when your option could've been to calmly say what needed to be said to the guy who made the error, come to agreements designed to make sure it didn't happen again, and then…(here's the real key)…move on. Getting stuck in our downward spiral of rage, stuck in the story we've spun, is the surest way toward unnecessary suffering.

At times like these, it pays to remember the old carpenter's motto: The difference between a good carpenter and a poor one is a good carpenter knows how to fix his mistakes.

Fix it. Forget it. Move on.

**To Everything There Is a Season**

Coinciding with this passage from Ecclesiastes is the Buddhist tenet of *impermanence*, which acknowledges that life has within it suffering; that the reason we suffer is because of our mental and emotional attachments to the people, places, things, and outcomes of this life's experience; and that these circumstances are continuously changing. Whether it's love, career, money, children, marriage, you name it, it is all going to change. And when we're attached to it looking a particular way, we suffer.

One of the strategies in dealing with these disappointments is to learn to detach, mentally and emotionally, from the struggle that often accompanies pain. As we gain confidence in identifying and then detaching from the struggle, we practice detaching from the attachment itself. When we come to understand that life has an ebb and flow of impermanence to it, that the fundamental dynamic of life is change, the good stuff as well as the bad stuff, we develop a kind of resiliency to suffering we did not have before. In this way, we are ultimately happier, because we aren't defining our happiness by exterior circumstances but by our frame of understanding.

**Suffering Through Life**

Have you ever known anyone with an aura of Eeyore? Remember Eeyore the donkey from *Winnie the Pooh*? People like this always seem to find the dark cloud on a sunny day. Their demeanor can change the vibe of any room they walk into.

In fact, we all have the potential for Eeyore Thinking at points in our lives. Should there be those days when we find we have brought it into the room, we have the power to catch ourselves, step away for a moment, and reset the day into a higher-thought realm of compassion and equanimity. When we keep our eye singularly on the good around us, seeming difficulties slip away. Our worldview is shifted and lifted into a new way of being and operating in the world, which comprehends that, in spite of pain, suffering is optional.

Now, I'm not promoting the idea of playing "let's pretend" here. There is some painful stuff that goes down in everyday living, to be sure. A health diagnosis comes in. A customer won't pay you. Your mate asks for a divorce. Your kid wants to go to USC, and you can't afford it. Intergenerational traumas, like addiction or the experience of racism, raise their heads. These are all very real challenges in life with very real pain, and they spare no one's socio-economic status.

In my own house growing up, when dealing with pain or disappointment, we were sometimes encouraged to, "offer it up to the poor souls in Purgatory." This may be fine when cut from the JV volleyball team, but how effective a remedy is this going to be for bullying, sexual harassment, shaming, abuse, or discrimination?

That stuff is real, and often real painful.

Perhaps, some of the less weighty stuff can be dealt with over a few beers, but the deeper stuff is not going to be so easy to shrug off. It may even take working with a therapist to heal it, so it no longer adversely affects our life and the choices that go with it.

And yet even with real pain and trauma, have you ever noticed there is the pain of a challenge or difficulty, and then there is the suffering we can slather on top of the pain? That's the suffering part. We have a choice in that part. It is often not easy to do, but once we can name what the difficulty is with accuracy, we can then take the steps necessary to shift and lift the thinking around the difficulty. With consistent practice, and vigilant self-honesty, we may not actually eliminate the condition, but we can definitely release the power the condition once had over us. And we are free! The folks who practice living in this way are living life on purpose. They are living consciously.

### The Difference

The difference between people who live from an inner knowing of the personal power of conscious living and those who do not is obvious to anyone who is the least bit observant. It is that powerful. I don't know if living consciously is something busy working people give much thought to. Often, all they are aware of is a sense of low energy or inner discontentment, sometimes for so long it feels normal.

They may even believe there is value in suffering, specifically with a payoff in the afterlife.

What I know for myself, and many others, is when we practice the art of living consciously, we find that not only does life get easier, but we also intuitively draw to us the right clients, the right workers, and friendships that are dynamic and supportive. Our health and energy level are super-sized because we are no longer burdened by the heavy lifting of self-inflicted suffering.

Now, I know we can all think of some pretty nasty scenarios where this may appear not to be true, but ultimately I'm sure all would agree, regardless of circumstance, we can live in the sweet spot of life when we release the idea that there is any value in suffering.

From the deathbed to the truckbed, any condition of life can be shifted to the better when we apply the power of living consciously to the mix.

## Too Busy to Be Effective

I think it's a given that there are countless ways in which we experience suffering. Some conditions are easier to manage spiritually than others. One of the ways we can suffer in life is when we feel trapped by the calendar. This is one area conscious living addresses almost immediately. Ultimately, we must realize we create the calendar to start with.

Can we take a moment and acknowledge we have very busy lives full of all kinds of distractions? Where our parents may have had a stay-at-home spouse to hold down the fort, today both parents are working. The pace of work has accelerated tremendously. The smart phone is a wonderful innovation that also includes messaging service, calendar, and so much more. Yet, like the calendar, we must be careful to make the phone the servant rather than the master. In short, we live today in a very busy and easily distracting culture. Never has there been a more crucial time to learn to center ourselves to and create some space in our lives.

For myself, I have found each day is most effective when I start it with ten minutes of quiet time, where I simply take a moment to focus on my breath and settle my thoughts.

You may be thinking, "Who has time for that?"

Well, back in the days of being Construction Guy, I would arrive to the site early, lay my seat back so the crew wouldn't bother me, and set the phone timer for ten minutes. The result, invariably, was clearer thinking and better effectiveness.

Interestingly, the way I proved this to myself was when I wasn't in the quiet-time practice. I discovered its value while noticing how much less I accomplished when I missed my morning ritual: More miscommunications, more errors, less tolerance with my workers or homeowners, usually in the form of internal mental tempest. Pass the Rolaids!

Unfortunately, it could also leak through my outside voice. The results might've been hilarious if they hadn't been so emotionally and financially costly.

So, ten minutes out of a 24-hour day is just about the smallest and easiest investment we can possibly make for such a profound shift in how well we have the potential to make our lives work for us. This principle has a high rate of return.

### Damn the Torpedoes

I get that some days we just have to lower our head, put our shoulder to the cart, and say, "Damn the torpedoes! Full speed ahead!" I know sometimes I can overthink something to death. Living consciously does not mean living in your head. When I used to work remodel jobs as a lead carpenter, I often encountered situations or conditions that were unexpected and unplanned for; often, it was a situation the architect could not have foreseen. An example of this is when, say, an important structural beam intended to support the new roof structure was found to contain termites. This can be a challenging and complex problem to deal with in real time. As a young carpenter, I could stand there half the morning staring at the challenge, trying in my mind to allow for every variable, trying to build the thing in my head, nail by nail, searching for the fastest and safest solution. With years of experience, I ultimately learned it was important to simply do the next indicated thing. By doing what was right in front of me, with everything else shed away, the situation got simplified, as I would then be directed to the next indicated step. Because, after all, we cannot build the whole thing in our head.

Sometimes thinking is not building; building is thinking. What do we know? What don't we know? Damn the torpedoes! Full speed ahead!

### Slave to the Schedule

Let's think more about this calendar thing for a moment. With further consideration of our working life, from the perspective of self-inflicted pain, we know there's the stuff we feel we *can* do something about, and then there's everything else. Our schedule is just such a place.

At first glance, our calendar may look as if it's driven by outside influences, and we appear to be powerless over it. Yet, if we are honest with ourselves and take responsibility for what's on the calendar, upon closer examination it should be self-evident we are the ones setting the calendar and no one else, and the idea of being slave to the schedule is a self-created construct. When we understand and know this to be true, we become the master of our schedule, the master of our own destiny, and this is a very powerful way to live.

To seize our power away from the calendar, it's important we learn to do two things:

First, learn to say NO.

Secondly, and perhaps even more crucially, learn to be pessimistic rather than optimistic about time-estimate commitments.

For instance, there is good science now that measures the factors of what drives people to be chronically late. Discounting those who seemingly just don't care that people are waiting on them, it turns out the chronically late are often overly optimistic about how long it takes to get from A to B. The fact that you made it to the golf course in fifteen minutes for an 8:00am tee time on Sunday morning doesn't mean you're going to get there on a Monday at the same time. Especially if you're on the 405 Freeway!

What researchers have found is we tend to generalize broadly that which was a unique one-time experience. The *one time* you made it in fifteen minutes, making all the lights, with no traffic, becomes the rule rather than the exception.

It's something to consider in determining what you can fit into your schedule, and what, from a practical and reasonable standpoint, you may not be able to.

In this way, we stay free of stress, which makes it possible to think about the task at hand rather than stressing about the future.

### Make Time to Take Time — In the Truck?

To live our most effective life, we must Make time in order to Take (or even Create) time. It may seem counter-intuitive, but I have found I am most effective when I start my day with a quiet session. As I stated earlier (I guess I can't state it enough), ten minutes out of a 24-hour day is a pretty small investment to make for such a profound potential shift in how effective our day can work for us. We are, after all, looking for ways to make our lives work rather than not work, correct? And I submit, you wouldn't be reading these pages if you already had that dilemma licked.

So, let's consider, practically, how we can set aside ten minutes each day to unplug.

Years ago, before the smart phones of today, I made a meditation CD with ten minutes of serene music on it. I wanted to be able to do this quiet-moment thing without watching the clock, because I've never lifted one thought or burden by clock-watching. Today, every smart phone has a timer and a stop-watch on it, so you don't have to go through the pains of making a CD.

Next, you need a place to retreat to during the workday, so you can do this. For years, I used my truck. My crew knew not to disturb me during that time, because I established the boundaries I needed. Eventually, with consistent practice of quiet contemplation, I learned I could do this anywhere. Today, I know to look for places to meditate because I know I'll always experience the benefit. Believe it or not, I even once meditated at the DMV, waiting and waiting to be called even though I had an appointment. Here's what resulted: It made the time go by faster; I was not a resentful SOB when my name was finally called; and the clerk and I had a wonderful experience of peace, harmony, and Right Action at the DMV!

That was a good day. And all because of my meditation practice. I made time to take time. And the time was used well.

## Finding Our Way Through a Busy Day

Conscious living with an effective calendar and realistic schedule can begin to nudge us into greater productivity, even when there is the space to say *No* within it. It's like swimming in a river. Knowing it is pointless to swim against the current, we can change direction and move forward with purpose. When we are living consciously, and these preliminary tools of creating a realistic calendar are in place, we find there will even be times when we can simply tread water for a while, and let the current itself push us along with little effort.

"Go with the flow, man" ain't just for hippies anymore!

Okay, so now we've explored this idea of starting the day with some quiet time. This quiet time is slowly but surely training our minds to be present, to be *right where we are*. This means as we are moving through our day, we are fully present with the task at hand. The point is to shift our minds from ruminating on what did or didn't happen earlier (the past) and scheming about what to do at the next appointment (the future) to, instead, being fully present with this moment—which is the only thing in life that's real anyway. The past and future are simply our imaginations running amok, without the calming reassurance of our conscious mind.

Staying with the river metaphor for a moment, it's easy to allow ourselves to be trapped in a back eddy with the flotsam of rumination, or jet through the rapids, never seeing the dangerous boulders ahead. When we are fully present, we are much more likely to make conscious choices. And often, we even find the unconscious choices working in our favor when there is flow-versus-resistance operating in our daily lives.

Mind you, we're not simply skimming the surface of this flow of life. We're not inner-tubing with a case of beer in tow. That's called vacation. We're in the flow. It's really more kayaking than inner-tubing. We might even get flipped over, at some point, but we can right ourselves, for we are using forward momentum to our advantage. We set our line, and we follow it.

Now, here's an important distinction. We're also not cruising. Cruising is much too passive for conscious living. I have personally found cruising through life to be a subtle foe, in that it has great potential to lull me into complacency. And please understand, I'm not saying we don't need to rest, because in fact when we rest, and know we are resting, the time can be deeply restorative. Cruising, on the other hand? We need to make sure that's not simply procrastination in a new skirt.

Have you ever noticed how when you're doing something you like, there are not enough hours in the day? Conversely, doing something difficult can make an hour feel like a day?

One of the areas I would encourage you to look at in your schedule is the time you spend doing anything other than the task at hand. If you can recognize this behavior in yourself, welcome to the Procrastinators Club. We'll have our first meeting as soon as we get around to it!

In my own life, I have to do two things around this tendency. 1) Acknowledge I do it. 2) Break tasks down into smaller segments. This can be as small as minutes long. For instance, I wrote this book by writing in six-minute increments, with timed breaks for distractions. And guess what? In time, this seemingly impossible task got done.

## Building Momentum

By now you can sense I'm using the calendar to help identify the ways in which we often get in our own way, and how these unconscious habits of "there's never enough time" are often obstacles to our most effective life and what's best for us.

The calendar can be the path to suffering, or it can be the path to ease and grace.

You might even call it the *critical path*. Where, in construction or other management projects, this can be a structured plan, what I'm really referring to here is realizing the momentum present in our day, and seizing it. Momentum is the hidden power propelling us through the day, and it actually adds to our productivity. It is the very current I was referring to earlier.

When we look for it, and seize it, we will find ways to use momentum to our advantage. We are no longer merely going with the flow; we are intuitively directing it.

Using the kayak idea, we are now steering ourselves through the flow of the day instead of being steered, because our lives are not set in concrete. And suffering is optional.

# What's in Your Chapter 1 Toolbox?

In Chapter 1, we've just explored the challenges of daily living. We've learned we are masters of our own destiny, and we're curious to discover who is truly at the helm. We need to stop, take time to observe our life situation, take inventory of what works and what doesn't, see what (or who) stands in the way, and know there is a solution to all of life's challenges.

It's time to create your Materials List. What do you know? And what do you need? Get your pencil out, and take a moment to answer these questions before moving on to Chapter 2.

1.  What are the factors in your life that really make you excited to get out of bed in the morning?

_____
_____
_____
_____

2.  What situations in life do you find the most frustrating?

_____
_____
_____
_____

3.  Is there anything going on where you ask yourself, "What's the use?" And if so, what are these activities that make you feel trapped?

_____
_____
_____
_____

4.  Once you have your answers to the above questions, are you now ready to do something about it? _____!

# Chapter 2
# Reset the Forms

While I understand we all have challenges, it is important to remember that challenge need not define your life. There are no rules requiring you to live the life you lived yesterday, last week, last year, or even the last ten years.

I have seen people live life with frustration and futility written all over them, and they didn't even know it. We don't know what we don't know—until we know it. *I know* because I was one of those guys.

I remember while in the middle of my own struggle, my dad looked at me one day, shaking his head, and speaking in that soft Irish brogue. "Son," he said, "your life is like the wheel of the manure spreader. It's just one continuous round of shite." There was truly no judgment in his comment; just a sad observation.

Ironically, this was my own twisted understanding of something we heard as kids when faced with a struggle that was, in part, keeping me stuck in the spray of manure; back to that ole "offer it up for the poor souls in Purgatory" thing. Can you see how deeply ingrained it was? I actually believed there was some kind of heavenly pay-off to bearing my earthly suffering. To be honest, I can't believe there are many today who see the world this way.

Let me say unequivocally, it is not necessary to suffer through life in order to get to heaven. As stated earlier, the essence of Buddhist teaching revolves around the nature of suffering. The Four Noble Truths, in a nutshell, say that suffering exists, and that there is a clear and workable path through it (hint: it has to do with that idea of non-attachment). Suffering does not have to be the mantra for your life. In fact, as long as you keep telling yourself your life is one endless grocery list of suffering—brother, it shall be!

I ask you right now to consider the idea that heaven and hell are not literal places, but rather places in the mind, ways of thinking, which either raise us up or keep us locked in a dungeon of dysfunction, fear, reactivity, and playing small in life, in ways that feel like torture.

When we experience life as struggle (and we *will* have those moments; we're beautifully, imperfectly human, after all), we must ask ourselves how we got here in the first place. If we are truly being honest about it, it has been our own thinking, or lack thereof, that has created our reality. Not the government, the boss, or that A-hole customer who won't pay us. These may be contributing factors, but ultimately, it's what we think that keeps us stuck or sets us free, despite exterior circumstances. Knowing this to be true, what are we prepared to do about it? What is ours to do?

## We Set Our Own Rules

To that end, let's take a moment to check in. How was your day yesterday? What were you like as you went about your business? Were you productive and effective? The picture of serenity and peace? Doling out wisdom and encouragement at every turn? Or were you pissed off and angry? Snapping at your buddies, spouse, kids, having social media wars with total strangers? Were you a slave whipped by your schedule? Was it a one-step-forward-two-step-back kinda day?

String a few of these latter ones together, and you have the recipe for burnout. When days turn into weeks of this, you've officially entered a rut. And although we can all find ourselves in these ruts once in awhile, we certainly don't need to move in and furnish it.

*Yea, though I walk through the valley of the shadow of death ... I just don't need to move in and furnish it!*

I think people often forget (or perhaps have never known) we are masters of our own destiny. We set the schedule, make the appointments, and make those commitments in our family life. We cannot predict the outcome, and stuff can and does happen, but we absolutely have the power at our disposal to shave those odds significantly with our intentions and actions, and ultimately learn to cultivate a steady, reliable inner peace even when the shit hits the fan. Every day, we are making dozens of small choices, which, taken together, demonstrate our ability to live in a conscious way and in the overflow of life. How is this true for you today?

### How Did I Show Up Last Week?

When we want to effect real change in our lives, it becomes imperative to stop and see where we are. With Google Maps, GPS can tell us exactly where we are, but imagine trying to use Google Maps without first knowing your starting point; it doesn't work. In order to use life's GPS (Generally Positive Stuff), we are going to have to turn away from all of the distractions, whether it's ESPN or social media, and just be still for a few moments.

In assessing where we are in life, we not only have to check the to-do list, but we also have to see how we're feeling about life in the broadest sense. If you're a dude reading this, you probably know this is something we're not very often good at. Hell, most guys may not even think in such ways, let alone have the language to put words to such things. Relax. There's no need for therapy quite yet. We can make it easy by simply reflecting on our life, and by asking ourselves, "Does this situation make me feel Mad, Glad, Sad or Rad?"

Most emotions fall under these four categories, and this will be enough to get you started. It doesn't take much time. Five minutes tops with practice. Why not stop reading for a moment and try making your list now? Compile a handful of situations in your life you're presently dealing with. Then assign each one an emotion from the prior page.

### Who Do You Want to Be?

Welcome back! Now that you have your Mad-Sad-Glad-Rad list, ask yourself, in the context of this list, "What kind of person does this list make me? And how different is that from the person I *want* to be?"

My preference is to feel Rad, even as I know it's probably not reasonable most of the time. Personally, I actually do find myself in this space more often than not. And that ain't bad!

It's also important to answer this question of who you want to be from YOUR perspective. Not from your spouse's, partner's, the Rotary Club's, employees', or even your kids'.

Keep in mind, this exploration is for you; no one else need see it but you, so tell the truth. There is no gain in being in denial about it nor any punishment for being honest. When looking at this aspect of yourself, think about the things you really like and appreciate about yourself. Don't be surprised if this is a bit tricky. You may not be accustomed to tooting your own horn. But you're not tooting here—*unless you had a burrito for lunch*—you're taking inventory of the ways you show up in life that make you feel comfortable in your own skin and allow you to operate in integrity.

We all have a self-image of who we would *like* to be—if we had the powers of a superhero and could instantly transform ourselves—*that* guy (or gal). Make that list. Next, toss out all the stronger, leaner, taller body-image stuff. What are the qualities that inspire the items on your list? Examples: confident, articulate, heroic, tender, kind-hearted. That kinda stuff. Keep in mind, you may not be this person yet; it's the person you'd like to be.

### Set the Tone

From the perspective of having explored who you want to be in the world, now make a list of the ways you actually DO show up. How do those things line up with your first list? If you're honest and diligent with this process, you'll be able to spot the ways in which you don't quite show up. This list is an inventory that should be taken in the same way a shopkeeper takes inventory to see what's been sold, kept, or even stolen. This is a fact-finding mission, not ammo to beat yourself up with. You see, the ways we don't show up actually point to the solution when approached from an inventory perspective.

If you look closely at your lists, you will undoubtedly see that some of the differences between how you'd like to show up versus how you actually do (or don't) are often influenced by external factors, which nonetheless shape us in unconscious ways. Factors such as race or ethnicity are obvious ones, but there are so many others. And some of those may have created biases or limitations, which have now become so crammed into your subconscious you have simply accepted them as law. Everything from what you eat to what's eating you!

Perhaps there is nothing you can really identify specifically; you're just feeling tired.

*Sick and tired of being sick and tired.*

Maybe life feels bigger than you can handle on a day-to-day basis, driven by a perception of not having any control over your circumstances. Your choice is to create your life of tomorrow from the power of conscious thought today. What you think today creates your tomorrow. To live your most effective life, you have to be the driver, not the passenger. Your power of choice today brings a measure of control for tomorrow.


## The Wheel

"Boy, your life is like the wheel on the manure spreader; it's just one continuous round of shite!"

So, speaking to the self-inflicted pain of over-committing and over-extending, or the influence of unrecognized biases, or just plain screwing things up, I again recall the day my Irish father, in watching me move from chaos to calamity, made that statement to me.

I remember the sting of those words even today, some 30-plus years later. And I was no boy then; I was a grown-assed man! But it certainly was accurate. So, of course, I did what any 30-year-old married man would do—I blamed it all on my wife.

*Yeah, I know.*

I will say this though; it did, in spite of my immaturity and arrogance, serve to wake me up to the fact that my life wasn't working. It wasn't instant, this dawning. In fact, even though I knew my life wasn't working, I still wasn't quite ready to consider a solution. At first, I just kept spinning the story in my brain that my life was a fun party with a few problems. Clearly, I needed to experience the continuing shit-storm of drama for a few years more, before I was ready to grow up.

It's all really just about whether or not we're ready. And until we truly are, no significant shift in consciousness will ever be made.

Let me say that again.

Until we are truly ready—to be vigilantly honest about ourselves and the challenges to our character—no significant shift in consciousness can ever be made.

## Wheel of Drama

Another indicator of how we're doing in life is to take stock of the level of drama swirling around the flow of our day. Drama is great for driving the story of Westeros and the Night King in "Game of Thrones," but do we really want that kind of drama in our life?

Slaying dragons all day long is pretty exhausting, whether of our own creation or not.

Every day, with every thought, behind every action, I want to create a storyline of victory, one day at a time. No dragons please!

No backstabbing sub-plots with the betrayal and anger that go with them. Not to mention, questionable relations with my auntie!

What I do want is to live happy, joyous, and free. How about you?

### Wheel of Dharma

So, now, instead of Drama, let's talk about Dharma.

Dharma is a term used in Indian philosophy to describe cosmic law-and-order, which includes duty, conduct, virtue, and the way to "right living." Its equivalent in Judeo-Christian thought might be The Word, as describes biblical law. Bottom line; it's the truth of life and living, and our most potentialed role in the Grand Play.

The purpose is to have awareness of the realities of daily living, and, especially from the Buddhist perspective, to develop an awareness of the futility of engaging so much with "stuff." To most westerners in the throes of acquisition, wealth, and power, this may neither make any sense nor be very enticing.

To such a person, I ask you to be willing to consider, for just a moment, that blindly surrendering to behaviors of conquest never serves you in the long run. Because it never ends. There's always another hill beyond the horizon.

And it's not only wealthy captains of industry who engage in power trips; overbearing managers, business owners, and even married couples engage in power struggles all the time. This is an effort that often leads to capitulation, sure, but rarely does it lead to cooperation and harmony, free of resentment. As a result, it is usually futile.

When you become willing to see life as it really is, and how you really are, rather than how you dream it to be, replete with Dr. Evil visions of ruling the world, only then can you begin to figure out what to accept and what to change, and then take responsibility for what is yours to do.

THAT's the moment you'll be living your Dharma versus your Drama.

**No Victims, Only Volunteers**

Finally, when we understand we truly do create our own reality, we have a choice to make. We can either live life from a passive, victim-mentality way of thinking or from an active and dynamic way of thinking. And with an understanding that we are always creating our experience, we now have a personal investment in riding the wave.

It's a harsh thing to say, and even more so to realize, but in life there are no victims, only volunteers. This can be disheartening in the moment and may actually require some time to ruminate and meditate on, before moving forward with this text. So, take the time, if you need. Because, this dawning IS the point of power. The point of leveraging Right Thinking into a new way of living. And that's huge!

# We Create Our Own Reality

We've now hammered away on this idea that we are responsible for our own life. Next, how do we make it different? Setting aside the to-do list for a moment, consider some of the things you know as a working person.

I suppose this could depend on what kind of work you do. This calls to mind the old joke/question: What do you need to know to be a plumber? The boss is an SOB, payday's on Friday, and shit flows downhill. Oh, and *parts is parts*. You gotta know your parts.

Generally speaking, though, there are things all working people have in common. They have to show up at a regular time. They have a boss, either a manager or a customer. They don't set their own hours. It appears working people are subjected to all kinds of influences out of their control. But is this really so?

The truth is, we are in control of the whole deal. We can choose to be an ordinary worker, or we can choose to be exceptional. The wonderful truth of this observation is we all have exceptional within us in spite of bitchy bosses, crabby coworkers, or wretched working conditions. We can be exceptional in spite of the world of conditions. What would being exceptional look like to you? If you need a hint, take a look at the inventory of good you created a few pages back.

(And if you haven't already done so, this would be the cue to go back and get caught up with your inventory list before moving forward.)

By taking the time to do this work, we discover a truly empowering truth about life, whether in the professional or the personal realm. And that is, we have options! Options are possibilities. The truth of life is we live and move in a field of infinite possibilities for good. Yes, we must change our current course of action (or inaction), but our feet are not cast in concrete; our life is not cast in stone.

### The Wonder of Concrete

Let's talk about concrete for a moment, shall we? Pretty much everyone at some point in life has seen concrete being poured. Whether in watching street crews on the roadway, building a new walkway in the garden, or forming and pouring a foundation, if you think on it for a moment, concrete is pretty amazing stuff. It starts as fluid and assumes any shape we can think of. I have seen concrete cast into 50' tall sculptures, become a multi-story building, or formed and poured as a boat hull and floating bridges. Cement that floats on water? *Impossible!* you say.

So, yeah, concrete is some trippy stuff. It's made of cement, sand, gravel, and without reinforcement is pretty brittle. At the same time, concrete mixed properly can have a half-life of 90 years, meaning in 90 years it's still strong as hell! The Romans discovered this amazing building material 2,300 years ago, but its secret (meaning, the secret to making Portland cement) was lost until the 19th century. The Roman mix was so strong there are parts of Roman roadways still in use today.

So, what's all this got to do with anything? Well, concrete starts out as a fluid, then it sheds a little heat and goes rock solid. In fact, if you don't know what you're doing, it can kick off before you're ready for it, to disastrous results. Think on that for a minute.

There are all kinds of liquids that temporarily take on the shape they're poured into. Pour tequila and orange juice into a glass and it will assume the shape of the glass—until it's consumed. But with concrete, the liquid will hold the shape of the glass as a solid for a hundred years, and then some. That tequila sunrise ain't gonna make it till sundown!

## We Set the Forms

We have spoken to how concrete can assume any form we give it. For someone who is skilled in building the form, any shape is possible, bound only by the imagination of the builder. That said, one must have *some* understanding of what wants to be built. It's not enough to know I want to build "something." What is needed is a reasonably clear vision of what the end result is meant to look like and to bring focus and attention to the task of building the form needed to produce the result. What is needed is structure to contain the concrete with materials strong enough to contain the substance until it sets.

It is important to remember we want the form to be as straight, as level, and as true-to-plan as we can make it. In building a foundation in the physical world, this is crucially important, for everything that's built on it later is affected by the care, attention, and precision we have given to it.

The same is true for our internal foundation, the foundation of our thinking. The only difference is, when it comes to our thought foundation, straight and true may not necessarily be as apparent or obvious, and the next step can sometimes be unclear.

Can we be okay with this uncertainty? Consider how empowering it is to know when a new thought is needed. Think back before now on how easy it was to wallow around in futility, not knowing what the hell was going on. The good news is, unlike forms set in the material world, in the world of thought, we can have a new thought, and reset the forms as needed. This thought is not bound by anything in the material world. It is not bound to ways of thinking that have come before. In this way, thought is the form to which our life takes shape.

This is important to know because we want to empower this new thought with as much clarity, focus, even faith and belief, as we can muster. Because, as we already know, there are many distractions in the thought world that can stymy the best laid plans of mice and men.

### Substance Bound Only by Imagination

If we imagine life as a *thought world*, we can see how, just as concrete is the substance held in the materials we've built, *life* is the substance with which our thinking sets the form of the desired structure or result. Concrete is a substance that has uniformity to it and is bound by the physical laws in which it is used. Imagine *life* as substance—the logical result of the tendency of our thought materializing. And not as some kind of Jedi mind trick but as the logical result of our thinking. And, just as the shape of concrete is bound only by the static form it fills, so our thoughts create the limits of our life's form. Our thought, then, is bound only by our willingness to engage with imagination with as much courage as we can.

Perhaps you believe yourself to be not very imaginative? Not so! Every time you daydream, every time you think about her, every time you picture what you're going to do with your weekend, you're using your imagination—because the weekend hasn't arrived yet. You engage your imagination with the ease of a child, even when you think you don't. Imagination has no prerequisites; you need no formal education to use it. In fact, some would argue that education could be a block to imagination if all we've learned is how to regurgitate facts, figures, and numbers. That said, the educated mind that is also imaginative is the most powerful and innovative tool we have.

Without imagination, there would be no relativity. Einstein would be a blip in history rather than the catalyst for how we understand life today. Examining the smallest aspects of existence, he spoke eloquently about life as a kind of substance he called quanta, particles in a field of space/time, trippy concepts then and still today. Einstein himself spent the last decades of his life exploring the ways in which a unified field exists. Yet, he struggled to accommodate the "uncertainty principles" being explored by others. He seemed to have taken a determinist's view in the way he experienced life, and found quantum mechanics an impressive theory, *"…but hardly brings us closer to the secret of the Old One. I am at all events convinced that He does not play dice."*

And still, it was undeniably Einstein's imagination driving the world of physics during his lifetime. So much so that in applying Einstein's theories, and those subsequent to them, physicists today are sounding more like mystics than scientists. As more evidence is gathered, the idea that our thought creates our reality will be more than a fanciful notion, but rather an accepted idea by science as fact. Can life, as substance, be the quantum field?

My point is simply that imagination is a thought tool you and I can use consciously. To give attention to the wildest imaginings for our life, to give these imaginings a voice, is to step out of old ways of thinking that, up until now, may have held us bound. And with our imagination, we can take our first giant leap to freedom.

All that said, let us remember imagination without action is just fantasy. We start by thinking, yes. But that is only the beginning, not the end. It is the launching pad, not the landing strip.

# What's in Your Chapter 2 Toolbox?

In Chapter 2, we explored how experiences in everyday living are reshaped through engaging imagination with thought to create the life we want versus the life we get.

This chapter's exercise is to do a little role-playing. If you were the Big Boss, where all situations and circumstances of the world must bend to your word and decree …

1.  Name three ways your working life would be different.

_____

_____

_____

_____

2.  Name three things in your relationships, both personal and professional, that would be different from how they are now?

_____

_____

_____

_____

3.  Name three things in the area of your health you would change.

_____

_____

_____

_____

4.  Name three projects you would love to do, if you knew you had all the time and money to carry them through.

_____

_____

_____

_____

# Chapter 3
# What Do We Know?

*What do you mean it's my thinking that created this mess? That's a load of jive! My life is a struggle because my customer won't pay me! My spouse spends too much money! My workers are stupid or don't care enough!*

While all of these conditions in your life may be true, I ask you simply, what is the common denominator within all of these factors?

In each one of these scenarios, can you identify how you chose (actively or passively) to allow these challenges to emerge as your life? Can you see any way in which you feel defined by your challenges and limitations rather than by your strengths? (Don't forget the questions you just answered in your toolbox!)

Let's remember, human beings are thinking beings. Not only are we thinking beings, we think about thinking. Thinking in this sense does not exclude other animals from having some level of intelligence. There are days when my dog is definitely smarter than me! And dolphin intelligence has been evidenced for years now. Having said that, I'm not sure dolphins consider the nature of water and its meaning to existence, but humans certainly do ask themselves, "Why am I here? And what does it all mean?" We've been doing so since antiquity.

The now famous dictum, attributed to Socrates, "The unexamined life is not worth living," begs consideration. Only you can determine if this is true for you as well. You can make the time for self-examination or not, but if you are to live your best life now, you need to learn and define who and what you truly are, warts and all. Not as some fractured composite of opposing values, but to see yourself as a unified person with both light and shadow aspects in personality. In time you may find the one you've discovered within yourself is generally a pretty good guy or gal. As you let go of some of that self-judgment, you'll find you can roll with others much easier as well. There's magic in this insight, for when humans sense we are one with all of life, we begin to see life as a continuum of connectedness; we are all in this together. And by focusing light onto our own shadow, we enlighten the world along with ourselves.

# Jive Talking!

We've all heard the expression, *you can't bullshit a bullshitter*. Whereas this may be so, I would add my own little tagline. *You can't bullshit a bullshitter unless he's bullshitting himself!*

In 12-step, it's often said, "You can always tell an alcoholic, but you can't tell him much!"

Human beings have wonderful imaginations, and we can create wonderful little jailhouses in which to do time. We talk ourselves into and out of all kinds of things, even using the idea that it's "God's will" to pursue that job (or that girl!), which may or may not be in our long-term best interest. Simply put, this is self-delusion, and people use it all the time to justify every manner of BS. It is part of the human condition. The dude Siddhartha pointed this out 3000 years ago.

Delusions come in all shapes and sizes. There is no one-size-fits-all. And everyone has them, so there's no need to beat yourself up about yours. In fact, if you have discovered them within yourself, this should be celebrated for the courageous act of self-inquiry and self-discovery it is. Unfortunately, it's usually the nature of self-delusions to have other people pointing them out to us, which is a real drag. Take my word for it! Should this happen to you, and you're not ready to look at it yet, simply say, "you may be right" and move on. Of course, there's also the modern euphemism for the f-bomb: "What-ev-er!"

## Being Open to Reality

All this discussion is simply to point out that in using the power of our thought to effect real change for good, it becomes imperative that we sift the bullshit from the ice cream. We must look at the ways we can deceive ourselves into taking a course of action simply because we forget that our perceptions shape our reality, and our desires for a particular outcome can shape our perceptions. This is an important insight, for only with this realization about life can we bring the power of awareness to our thinking.

And here's the coolest part. Should our last "brilliant" thought not work out as planned, we can always choose a new thought again. And again … and again … and again, if necessary, to produce the desired result.

If we really pay attention to the process, we become aware of the tendency of our thinking. It is the tendency, as well as the tenacity, that produces results. Thinking that one perfect thought *once* just ain't gonna do the trick. Consistent mental focus, over time, demonstrates itself in our life. So, let's make sure those thoughts are thoughts that warrant our attention; thoughts that are creative, dynamic, and with the energy of inspiration to ensure focus. This kind of thinking takes some measure of imagination. We need to engage our imagination to create our best life now.

## Imagination Is More Powerful Than Knowledge

Posted on the wall in my office is an Einstein quote: *"Imagination is more important than knowledge."* Knowledge is often connected to book learning. Book learning is something many working people may not have the resources for, or don't have time to do, or maybe don't even care to do. Happily, imagination is not exclusive to book knowledge. If it were, our childhoods would have been a real drag!

Is it not true, knowledge can sometimes lock us into modes of thinking that keep us bound to what we think we know, rather than encourage us to explore ideas yet to be tried or even given voice to? To break old ways of thinking that have us boxed in we have to be imaginative. We need to ask ourselves questions that require us to explore "what if" scenarios that reach beyond the current limitations of how we think life *must* be to what it *can* be. Examples:

*What if I'm smarter than I think I am?*

*Who would I be if...?*

*What if I had stayed home that night?*

*What if money was no object, and success was guaranteed?*

## The Delusion of God's Will

From the perspective of engaging in the power of thought, let us speak to how ideas of God can get in the way of our most effective life, unless and until we bring consciousness and awareness into our spiritual belief system. It's not my intention here to pick on religion, but rather to pick on the way many practice religion. I think there are questions worth asking ourselves:

*What if God is a much bigger idea than I think it is?*

*What if God is good and only good?*

*If I have an idea of salvation, does this idea release me to my most effective life?*

*Does my understanding of God keep me playing small and willing to accept the crumbs instead of the whole loaf of the bread of life, because I believe in an afterlife where "all things shall be added unto [me]"?*

I confess, the idea of settling for less in our life because *it's God's will* kinda makes me crazy. I'm not so different from others in this regard, as I lived life this way for years! And maybe it's because I was in my forties before I realized how much of my own life I was sacrificing to others (employers, customers, the church, etc.), to the detriment of myself and my family.

For years, working people have been told by society, directly or indirectly, that they are less than, or are made to feel they are not worthy because…

If you have a faith system consistently telling you how you don't measure up, you have a recipe for disaster, my friend. The God stuff, for good or ill, runs deep!

Now, I'm not a conspiracy theory guy here, but it doesn't take much to figure out that if you feel you aren't worthy, you are unconsciously setting yourself up for a fall. Again, I ask the question: What if God is good, and only good?

I am a carpenter by trade. My work is creative; I have come to see how satisfying this work can be. I know how it feels to appreciate the ability to make "a silk purse out of a sow's ear." I wonder if the Cosmic Creator of All would feel any less satisfaction? Would this Creator not delight in the creativity of that which has been fashioned in Its image and likeness to be creative? By most religious definitions, God is *the* Creator. Do we really think God is going to squash our attempts at creativity, or stand in the way of our demonstration of that Creative Power, because we get distracted by sex, drugs and rock n' roll? Is this not also part of the Divine Creation that man is? We may or may not discredit ourselves, but we cannot discredit the Divine.

If people need to utilize the concept of God's Will as a coping strategy to explain some calamity or heartbreak, that's fine, but to use it as an excuse for surrender rather than a rallying point to choose differently is not helpful.

There is a Creative Power at work here that requires our conscious direction. I think the notion of an Infinite Creative Power of the Universe, expressing as the thing it thinks about, is a powerful idea! Power we can use to change our life for good!

To consider that we can create in the same way using this creative power is a far more powerful expression of human life. In this way, our will allows God's will to create the life we want.

# The Common Denominator

By now, you have realized a most inconvenient truth—we are the common denominator in our own lives. No one else can live this life for us. If this were not so, I would go out and find a buff 30-year-old to go to the gym for me so I could have those six-pack abs I've always wanted. But alas, the gym does not work this way, and neither does life. If we are to live our most effective life, or even the life of our wildest dreams, we are going to need to acknowledge this truth that we are the common denominator in our life.

So, now, what do I mean by that exactly?

My math teacher used to go on and on about how "Math is life!" Well, let's see if that's true. Of course, those in the trades have learned this the hard way when learning to read a measuring tape. Fractions. UGH! I thought I'd left that behind in high school. In sixteenths no less! I thought my boss was gonna brain me the first time I relayed a measurement to him and said, about a block that was 13 9/16 inches, "It's 13 inches and one small line past the big line in the middle."

If you're a tradesman, you're smiling right now.

Let's look at what a fraction is, and how it really does relate to human experience. Take the fraction *1/4*.

This fraction can be called *one fourth*, *one quarter*, *1 over 4*; any of these designations would be correct. As you may recall, the number above (or in front of) the line is called the numerator, and the number below (or behind) the line is called the denominator. The number below the line is the one constant that defines the relationship, while the number above the line can vary. Whatever that top number is, it will always be defined by its relationship to the bottom number.

Or let's envision it another way. Imagine your life described as a circle with four segments. The circle is you, the denominator, the factor that never changes, and each segment of the circle represents aspects of your life: Health, Wealth, Creativity, and

Relationships. These sections are the numerators; they shift, change, appear, disappear, etc., all throughout our lives.

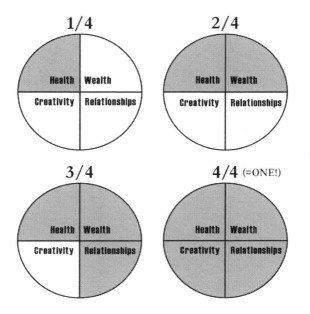

The minute one or more of those segments is lacking, the circle is out of balance.

Now, let's play with this observation for a bit. You have been taking some time with the toolboxes to break down small parts of your life and explore what works, what has struggle in it, and what has pain in it. Think of each of those parts as a slice from a pie. If you were brave enough in your explorations, you likely discovered *you* were the one consistent factor (the common denominator, the element that never changes). *You* had a part in everything.

Since our Common Denominator is the unmoved quotient, the interesting truth of this experiment is that we then draw to us the situations and circumstances on the numerator side of this fraction, that numeral *above* the line, meaning our situations, our circumstances, and our relationships, which can and do shift. And so, we may start at a 1/4, where only one segment of our life is really working well. But where we want to arrive is that intuitively aligned balance of Self. We want to reach 4/4. All quadrants working! And what is *four over four* in math? It's ONE!

## 4/4

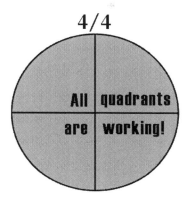

When we achieve balance, we demonstrate Oneness, and in the state of Oneness, Balance and Symmetry, the numerator and the denominator are interchangeable, for they are the same thing. Four over four, self over Self, self/Self. They are all ONE. And THAT is Power at work. The Power that runs through all of Life!

### Life Does Not Happen TO Us

The next idea in using the Power of Thought to effect change in our life is to understand a simple truth: *If I am responsible for my own life, if there are no victims, only volunteers, and if the Creative Power of the Universe is always working with me, then life is not something that happens TO me. If this Power works with me, I can direct this Power.*

Think on this idea for a moment. Do you feel more in control of your life knowing this Principle of Life is working for you by working with you?

### No One Can Do It FOR Us

Likewise, if you could hire someone else to live your most effective life, would you spend the money to do so? Call me crazy, but I'm going to go out on a limb and say you wouldn't. You've been making your way in this world by the strength of your body and by the power to think in ways outside of book-learning. I'm guessing that for the most part you, at least, like what you do, though perhaps you want more money and long-term security. The power of thought is a real thing. It's learning to pay attention to what you think, and to what you really want, rather than on what you don't want. This is a truly powerful way to shift your life for Good.

So, if not TO but FOR us, what's next? There is another component where practicing with thought is THE transformative Power of Life.

### Life Happens THROUGH Us

When we come to understand that this Thought Power can be directed with the power of choice, is it not self-evident that life happens through us rather than to us? This realization has real power in it, although the power is subtle. When we understand life happens through us, our perspective shifts and we become the observer of this power expressing as life. In this remarkable state, it feels as if time slows down, or becomes elastic, and projects are completed easily and on time. We begin to sense the world is working with us rather than against us, and the flow of life begins to feel like God's Will is, in fact, aligned with our own.

*"Ask, and it is given unto you."*

In this understanding of God, God's Will is to say YES! Only, we decide *what the ask is!*

When we understand that life happens through us rather than to us, there is nothing and no one against us except our own cracked thinking and skewed understanding of the world. And this has nothing to do with how much schooling we do or don't have.

History is full of uneducated geniuses and educated idiots. The only thing truly standing in our way is our own thinking! So, what do you say we choose wisely?

# You Are Not Your Challenge

Have you ever known, maybe even admired, someone who couldn't see how wonderful they were because of focusing on mistakes made earlier in life? Maybe they made a couple of whoppers, like a DUI or becoming a parent before they were ready. Perhaps they were simply an uninspired student, or received their degree in 17th-Century Irish literature instead of the business degree their father tried to interest them in (this is a quality problem, BTW). Having, myself, made a few mistakes along the way, I know how that feels. I also know the judgment and self-recrimination that goes along with it. How about you?

I had a realization about life several years ago that to me was subtle yet powerful. I am *not* the challenges that have presented themselves through my life; my challenges do not define me.

In looking back on my life, I've certainly made mistakes, but it's actually mind-blowing to think how harshly I judged myself about them. Then one day, I had this thought. "As long as I am locked into this narrow, negative way of thinking, I am looking backward and not forward." And it's not like anyone else knew what was going on. It's not like I was wearing a banner across my chest: "Follow me to Losers Anonymous."

Whether I am the captain of the high school football team, or a slacker hittin' the weed at lunchtime, I am not whatever old story I have of myself.

And neither are you.

Everyone has a past, and yes, we are responsible for whatever is in that story, but it no longer defines who we are; it's just a chapter in a story, a story we tell ourselves. How about this instead? *I am the author of my story. I can choose to write a new chapter at any moment of any day.*

Your business, your marriage, your children, a diagnosis, your bank account, none of these aspects of life defines you in totality. You are more than your life's challenges.

In your "I AM" story, there lays a field of infinite possibility available to demonstrate some cosmic something so much greater than the limited self. But we cannot find it if we are constantly looking back at our past misdeeds with unforgiving judgment. You are not your challenge, but the way you meet or don't meet those challenges can shape who you are.

### Past Wife Regression

It has taken me a lot of work to understand I am not my challenge, whatever that is, but particularly for me in relationships, both personal and professional. I use my own self as an example here because I don't think my life is any different from most. Generally speaking, I enjoy the life I have today. But once in a while, I allow myself to lapse into a Past Wife Regression. This is not helpful, especially considering my ex-wife could easily and clearly articulate all of the ways in which I did not show up in the marriage. Mind you, there is nothing my ex-wife could've said to hurt me had my thinking about myself been healthy and secure. But it wasn't.

And although I was fairly high functioning in many areas, I had a lot of uncertainty and fear around money issues, which meant I would not measure up.

I came to embrace this belief of *not-enough-ness* as being the truth about myself. I had created a life of struggle with its money problems and was looking to someone outside of myself to make me feel okay. That's a lot of BS to put on anyone, and yet couples do it to each other all the time, for all kinds of reasons.

Since our thinking creates our reality, how do you think that turned out? Did I mention I am her EX-husband? It took me a while to find my testicles after that one. Oddly enough, when I eventually came to my true self, I found them right where I'd left them.

Marital relationships are not the only place this dynamic can show up: The hard-ass boss, the obnoxious co-worker, even our weird Uncle Ned, who has managed to turn getting drunk at exactly the wrong time into an art form. Human beings are gonna have their stuff, and the closer we are with them, the more stuff is gonna happen.

I have found there are powerful wisdoms to glean from these kinds of experiences once you move beyond the hurt, anger, and maybe even shame. Whether being fired from a job or from a marriage, a lot of emotional baggage, even trauma, can be carried (okay, dragged!) behind us like an anchor chain.

At some point, these experiences need to make their way to the "*shit I don't want to forget for next time*" file. What goes in the file is what you learned—what you learned about yourself, your part, the things you *can* tolerate in other people and yourself, and the things you *can NOT* tolerate under any circumstances.

What have we learned about human nature in general? How can you and I be in the world taking less of life so personally? Perhaps pain can be a great motivator for getting our attention?

You see, with practice, we can learn to pay close attention to these kinds of mental exchanges. In time, we may even come to see that once in a while it's best to go through some short-term pain rather than to work within a long-term mistake. Not from a place of fear but of choice. The next time your gut is tingling, pay attention to it, and learn the difference between excitement and fear. Ultimately, we know we no longer need to create pain in order to learn, have, or be anything.

### Not Bound by Our Past

The power of thought is not bound by precedent. What has happened in the past should stay there. This cannot be stressed enough. In fact, as you play with the power of thought, you are going to discover all kinds of interesting physiological processes that happen at the level of sensation and brain activity.

For example, scientists using brain scans have found that if our thinking should wander over to the memory of some past hurt, resentment, or trauma, the brain doesn't know the difference between the memory of that trauma or if hurt is actually happening in real time. Crazy, right? Within the body, powerful chemicals are released that are triggered by the Fight, Flight, or Freeze response, even when we simply remember something, and which are the same chemicals released if we were threatened by a sabre tooth tiger! This stuff is in our DNA!

Fear is first. And when you become willing to consider the way in which this is true in your own experience, you learn to work with it and use it to your advantage. Name the fear, address it, speak up or walk away, but whichever you do, do it from a place of being okay with yourself, and being okay with what life is presenting you, and doing this in a conscious way.

The main thing is not to carry old hurts and resentments forward. It is wasted energy and always spills out in some other way, splattering on things that have no connection to the moment at hand. It is confusing and hurtful for all and can cost you plenty. There may have been a time when this was a winning strategy, or at least a coping mechanism, but no longer.

A wise man once said, "When I was a child, I talked like a child, I thought like a child, I reasoned like a child. When I became a man, I put the ways of the child behind me."

Living life in regression is a life lived looking in the rearview mirror. If we're looking backwards, we risk collision with what's in front of us.

## Demonstrate Your Highest Self

Considering the implications of the brain scan experiments, imagine the possibilities if we were to focus the brain on an intention for something in our life we would welcome, creating an affirmation of a yet to be realized goal.

If the brain cannot tell the difference between a real and imagined event, can we not see how this paradigm could be a powerful tool for accomplishing any goal we may have?

Let's examine for a moment what it might take for someone to increase the success of his business. Let's say this is our theoretical businessman's daily affirmation:

*I am attracting to me customers who appreciate value and pay me promptly. I call to me everything I need in order to sell 15% more in sales and increase my bottom line by 10% for this coming year.*

Considering the data from brain scans, if our businessman *acts as if* the goal is already accomplished, and he does this daily—this affirmation, this attunement of consciousness—before he knows it he is going to start engaging in the kinds of behaviors that allow his future goal to come to be.

Now, notice how he did not set his goals in some outlandish pie-in-the-sky way. What we don't want to do is play "let's pretend it's so." Instead, we are knowing it as already done, and then taking the action to make it so.

Henry David Thoreau said it stunningly.

*"If one advances confidently in the direction of his dreams, and endeavors to live the life which he has imagined, he will meet with a success unexpected in common hours."*

Working in this way is going to require us to stretch a bit, to exercise patience, and maybe a little bit of faith. We may be tempted to cut corners, to take shortcuts in order to move things along a bit faster. But it's crucially important we *not* succumb to this temptation. What we want is increase with no drop-off in quality. What we want is the calm faith in our business, our product, our goal, and not the manic desperation of the impatient and the insecure.

Which would you rather have? The reputation for being the cheapest guy in town, someone whom you can always get a deal off of because he has undercut his own belief in his product? Or would you rather have the reputation of being worth the wait and the extra money, because the quality of the product and the ease of the experience of working with you is such that folks see your value and are willing to pay a bit more?

That's what having a profitable company looks like, by the way.

Sometimes when considering how our thinking works, it's wise to go back to what we know. When I was a kid, I spent a lot of time watching cartoons. You could say I developed a kind of expertise around my favorite ones, quoting lines, chapter and verse. In those days, all of life's big riddles were addressed in cartoons.

Did you ever see the one with the devil and the angel? The tomcat is presented with an ethical dilemma—whether to clobber the pesky but cute mouse, or choose to be gentle instead. Suddenly, a little red cat devil with horns and a pitchfork appears on his shoulder and starts whispering in his ear, "Go for it! Take what you want!" Then poof! A little cat angel, halo and all, appears on the opposite shoulder, plucking a harp to raise him up and encourage him to forgo his baser cat instincts and do the right thing.

This metaphor still works for most of us today. Hundreds of times a day, we are faced with the choice, in business and at home, of whether to be harsh or kind. To take what we want and screw everyone else, or try and bring forth our best effort to allow our values of fairness and equality to shine through.

To propose the ways and means that create win/win scenarios that work for all concerned cannot happen in a vacuum. It requires you to be comfortable and confident enough in your own skin to allow the concerns of others to be considered. It makes you relevant and reputed because you have made the accommodations associated with fair dealing.

This is what principle is. And standards. It's also what compromise looks like, which is often necessary in business. Because, while there may be certain standards that absolutely cannot be compromised, for the sake of the product's value and maybe even its safety, a commitment to allowing the highest and best result for all is one principle that can get a lot of stuff done.

If it's going to be … it's up to thee!

# What's in Your Chapter 3 Toolbox?

In Chapter 3, we talked about delusions, and how the power of our thinking can work for or against us. We can use our thinking to advance our case. And we can use it just as powerfully to stay stuck in our little prisons and talk ourselves into, or out of, all sorts of things for the sake of our fears.

In the words of Dr. Maria Nemeth, from *The Energy of Money*, "Who are YOU willing to BE in order to live your BEST life now?"

Time to get the pencil out again before moving on to Chapter 4.

1.   Name three things you feel are standing in the way of your greatest good right now in career, special projects, or relationships.

_____
_____
_____
_____

2.   For the items you've just listed, what is it you believe needs to happen for these to work out the way you want?

_____
_____
_____
_____

3.   What concrete changes within yourself are you now willing to make, for your Greatest Good to present itself as your new reality?

_____
_____
_____
_____

# Chapter 4
# The Answer Is in
# Your Hands

Here's where we are so far. I have outlined some of the challenges to daily living. I have made the case for taking time to make time for engaging the power of thought in order to shift and lift your life into ways of thinking that up until now may have kept you feeling stuck. And I have encouraged taking personal responsibility in this arena, and employing rigorous, brave honesty about how you've tended to operate in the past.

Are there some things in your life you feel you have no control over at all? Where it feels like an impossible situation to you? I sure know I have. Maybe you've tried every conceivable remedy, only to be stymied by this and that from the success you've wanted so desperately to see in your life; the success you've been working ridiculously hard to achieve.

The good news is there is a way out of this seeming maze of challenge and futility. Armed now with what we've covered so far in this book, not only is there an answer; there is ample power in you to carry it out.

As a working person, you are already using this power on a daily basis, several times a day, in fact. It is a way of being in the world that is uniquely yours; defined by the attention, skill, and experience you bring to your work every day. It is the power behind your ability to fix things. It is the power that presents you with answers about why a building is out of square, why a product is not moving, or why an engine misfires. It is the power I know you have felt, even if only on the rarest of occasions, rolling out at the job site first thing in the morning. Maybe a day like the one I describe in the poem at the beginning of the book. It is that feeling of being one with all of life, in spite of the BS of daily living.

When we are in this place, it feels as if we can do anything. There is no situation or challenge we cannot meet. We are connecting to a source of power within ourselves we can use daily to build our business, grow deeper connections in relationships, access for creativity, even facilitate healing in our body. From retail workers to plumbers, hairdressers to welders, nurses, bookkeepers, and beyond, this power is always available and can never be depleted. It is a power that is everywhere present, contains all intelligence, and has enough juice to pull any vision of life into demonstration.

The only limitation is our thinking about it, and how it may not work for us. Ultimately, we need to take that recognition of limited thinking and shift it to allow the Infinite Power to work for us and through us, for our highest good and the good of others.

## Power You Can Use

At times, we experience this power as a sense of awe, beauty, majesty, energy, and connection. It is the space where in an instant everything suddenly makes sense, every hardship and challenge, every victory, every "I am Spartacus" moment, every loss or moment of grief experienced in a flash of insight, where you sense that all is connected, and that every moment of the past is linked to this present moment. This magical moment is connected to a field of Infinite Possibilities for Good, when we suddenly see the connections between the seemingly good and the seemingly bad. Because, it is all One Thing, expressing as our life, and a deep knowing sense that all is well in us. No matter the outward circumstance, we are one with a "right now" moment.

I had such an experience several years ago in my work truck, heading south on the 405 Freeway (the bane of the SoCal

51

commuter!). I looked up and saw the Getty Museum on my right. I could smell the fresh sprouting chaparral in the soft, early morning light. In a flash, I was transported to a sense of connectedness with all of life. It was an experience both transcendent and transformational.

I was suddenly aware that I was having a "moment" and consciously thought, "I have to hold on to this amazing insight and feeling!" And of course, the instant I thought it the moment was gone; it had dissolved right out of the present and back into the seat of my truck.

I've enjoyed a few of those moments in life.

## The Power of Awareness

There are actually a few things going on in this truck story. It happened during a particularly difficult time in my life. I had been exposed to a teaching that spoke to how to focus my thought and connect it to some Higher Power. I had been practicing keeping my thought focused in the present moment for a few weeks. I began to start my days with ten minutes of quiet. I turned away from the pain and challenge I was going through at the time and was focused instead on what was in front of me to do.

"I'm reading the blueprints. I'm directing the crew. I'm operating a saw. So, pay attention!" I'd say to myself. It sounds crazy now, when I think back on it. And practicing staying focused was, itself, distracting. Yet, within just a few days of intense practice, being actively focused on the flow of life actually started to become second nature. The crazy, hurtful stuff that had me so stirred up was still going on, but I was no longer biting the hook. Instead, I was just kinda gumming the bait in the way a wary trout does before successfully spitting out the hook and swimming safely away.

In this way, I began to notice more of life, my place in the flow of life, and all of the various actors and situations I'd called forth into my experience of life. I began to appreciate more. And in that appreciation, my mood shifted. I felt connected, alive, and aware. I was moving forward in the flow of life.

### Make Welcome the Magic

In that "I am Spartacus" moment, when I felt both inwardly connected and connected to all around me—MY life and the ONE Life, in a simultaneous union of deep insight—it felt like magic. In fact, it was weirdly magical and practical at the same time. I was in my Power! I caught the scent of something significant and mighty. Words failed me then, and at the same time, I knew intuitively that I had tapped a hidden wellspring of resource within me.

I've met many people over the years who have had the same experience in a similar fashion, yet each has been uniquely defined by his/her own experience of life.

And to be sure, what we all have in common is the desire for how to make welcome that experience again.

### Capture the Moment

So, how do we capture those moments? Perhaps Shakespeare posed the question best, when Hamlet asks, "To be or not to be?" When we have a peak moment like the one I've described, it's as if we've been awakened from a deep sleep, and once awake, we can't go back. There have been people throughout the millennia who have had similar, possibly even more intense, experiences. History calls them mystics, and mystics tend to be looked on as saints. Now, me? I'm more Ain't than Saint, believe me.

And just what is a saint or a mystic, anyway? I've certainly known people who are more "holy" than I. And I'm not talking about the *holier-than-thouers*; I'm not really interested in verbal testimonials or outward displays of piety. I'm talking about people whose vibe is peaceful and loving in spite of difficult circumstances. People who practice true humility to the point of being embarrassed to be exalted because of their faith. It would be logical to think clerics of any stripe are holy. Believe it or not, most would laugh at this presumption, even though their congregations may need them to be. After all, isn't that what people are putting money in the basket for?

In truth, it's the everyday folks who practice love and forgiveness who really get to me. I often think of my late Aunt MaryAnn in Ireland as being saintly. Her only miracle may have been to be loving and good-natured in difficult circumstances; but maybe this is enough to be a saint? I think it's far too easy to judge ourselves, or others, about such things. Maybe in the eyes of the Creator we are all saints striving to recognize this truth for ourselves? What would the world be if seven billion people knew they were all saints, made in the image and likeness of the Creator?

It also makes me realize my being an "Ain't" is anchored in an old belief system that should no longer be given so much power. And yet, to worry about being a saint or not is often just another distraction keeping us blocked from expressing the Infinite Power and Presence we are wanting to make welcome in our life.

Let's face it. Unless you were raised by wolves, you know what right and wrong is. If you don't know, the local District Attorney is happy to explain it to you: Keep your hands to yourself, be kind whenever possible, respect the property of others, keep your pants zipped up, pay your child support when due.

Pretty simple. It's in our DNA to know right from wrong. Yet, being human, we are going to fall short of the rules. And when we do, we pay the consequences.

There is an inherent Law of Life, a Law of Cause and Effect we're all subject to. And ignorance of the Law is no excuse. What if we know we're punished *by* our sins, and not *for* our sins? What if a sin is simply an error in thought?

I invite you to consider this for a moment. What if there's no judgment from God on High, but rather a Universal Holy Spirit and Intelligence always impressing Itself upon us and which responds equally to all of life as Love?

It's like we're swimming in the Spirit, like fish in water, wondering where the water is! How does it feel to imagine your life from this perspective of knowing the Divine?

You may be thinking, "Who am I to be considering such things?"

I say, "Who are you NOT to consider such things?"

## You Are the Expert

Here's a story about expertise. In January of 1994, I was a newly licensed building contractor operating out of the San Fernando Valley in the northern part of Los Angeles. This was mostly out of necessity, as the local area was suffering from a financial hangover following the real estate boom of the late 80's. Times were tough. I had two room additions going, which I'd gotten for a few points above cost. I did both for under 75K; cheap even in those days! I was concerned I wouldn't be able to support my new family. Then came January 17th, and the whole game changed in about three minutes' time as the Northridge earthquake leveled 20% of the local area. Paradoxically, along with the devastation of lost homes and lost lives came opportunity. My business grew five-fold in a year and didn't let up for the next three years. It's a disconcerting phenomenon having your business blossom in the wake of tragedy.

That said, I didn't make piles of money. Though there was a crazy influx of work to be had, as an entire community had no choice but to rebuild, there was a huge learning curve for me that ended up being very expensive. Every bit as expensive as any college education. At the end of a three-year hustle, I ran into a guy selling a computer system for maximizing earthquake insurance claims. He was selling a product, and the product was to negotiate on behalf of the homeowner as the contractor then turn the settlement over to said homeowner to do the construction himself. The negotiator would take 10% for overhead; the homeowner would get the 10% profit and the work. Totally legal, but it didn't feel right. I argued with the guy. "Ten percent for only doing paperwork?" It just didn't feel legit.

The computer geek asked me, "How much would you pay a lawyer to negotiate a car insurance claim for an accident?"

I knew 30% of a settlement was the standard lawyer's fee. And this guy knew I knew it.

"That's right!" he said. "Thirty percent for a lawyer. That lawyer is being paid for his expertise and experience. You'd be getting ten percent for your experience and expertise. Who do you think actually has more knowledge about negotiating an earthquake repair settlement? You or a lawyer?"

Where was this guy three years ago? The earthquake repair work in my local area had essentially dried up by this point. Most people had completed their repairs, except for a few diehard holdouts who didn't trust anybody—not insurance companies, contractors, or even family members. Who wants to work with people like that? I passed on the opportunity, but never forgot the lesson.

Who is the expert in the field of YOUR endeavors?

I think working people often lose sight of the value they bring to the lives of others. Everyone has an expertise they bring to the table on a daily basis. Whether a ditch digger or a landscaper, a carpenter or a retail worker, short order cook or delivery person, anyone who is striving to be the best at what they do in the most effective way is both an expert in their enterprise and a winner in life too.

Because, while book learning and education are important, a trained mind, regardless of whether attained behind the walls of academia or on the job and in the world, is powerful. Far more powerful than an untrained mind, to be sure! And within these working endeavors, there is a power expressing as that life and expertise.

To tap this hidden power effectively, we must be willing to stand in our expertise, free of boastful pronouncements, free of self-recrimination, and own that place in our thinking where we know what we are talking about, and we've paid our dues. To know there is nothing to earn and no debt to pay. The expert has arrived!

If we see ourselves as religious, we may even need to look at that. We need to examine the most basic beliefs, like sin. As suggested earlier, what if sin is not an offense against the Almighty, but rather, simply an error in thought? In this way, there is no sin but merely a mistake. Now, I don't mean to minimize it by saying "merely." Certainly, there have been situations in our lives (i.e., addiction, adultery) that are quite serious. But while the solution may not be easy, it is actually quite simple. We change our thought, and we change the tendency of our thought to the Good.

Shifting even this one idea can have a huge impact on the way we operate in the world. We begin to experiment with the idea that we are a co-creator with A Power Greater Than We Are Alone, choosing our way into a life free of limitation or constriction of any kind.

We are no longer subject to the slings and arrows of the statistical world of economies, divorce rates, even failing businesses. We ARE that outlier outside of the statistical norm. An outlier who is wildly successful in every way.

## You Matter

If you learn nothing else from this book, I want you to know there is no one else in the universe that is YOU. You are important! You are making your own unique contribution to the world in ways great and small. You matter! Just as your ancestors before you matter, for without them you would not be here. And just as YOU are the ancestor to people (and even ideas) who impact that which is yet to be.

You are more than what the world thinks of you. Your education, or lack of it, does not matter. Nor does your age, gender, clan, race, caste, or reputation. While these may have been aspects of you in the past, and may have shaped your life for good or ill, there is a *YOU* that is free of pretense or judgment. There is that place within you that has never been violated in any way. This *you* is the still, small voice whispering and guiding you intuitively toward solutions to problems, which present themselves throughout any given day. There are surface concerns in the world for sure, but there is a deeper truth of *you* beyond the cares and concerns of the day-to-day frustrations of life, and which is longing to express itself. It is the stillness behind the thinker. And it expresses itself to you throughout the day, if you are attuned to it.

It's that sense of connection you've felt working within your trade—that perfect day. We've all had those. It is the expression of an Infinite Power and Presence and Creative Force that is one with all of life. This power is not bound by any earthly thing, regardless of our thinking, religious denomination, or affiliation. It is experienced as an individual, and we experience it collectively when we come together in community, whether at a sporting event, rock concert, or a spiritual assembly. For me, this experience is what theologians of old call *the immanent and transcendent*. It is what people of faith call God. The experience of the One God expressing as Life through the many religions. This power is infinite and is everywhere present. It is intelligence, and it is its nature to create. It is bound by nothing but the nature of its own being, which is infinite. It is Love expressing as Life.

And being everywhere present, it is right where you are. In this way, all of creation is relevant, for it is an expression of this Creative Power creating all of life, making all of creation out of Itself. All of creation has the Creator in it. It all has value. Everything is a reflection of the Creator becoming the thing it thinks about. This includes you and me.

Given that you and I are thinking beings, what does this mean for us?

Consider the possibilities of living life knowing in some crazy way we're thinking with the mind of the Creator. How would our lives be different if we truly knew this to be so? How would life be different if we knew this for everyone and everything? You matter! … And so does everyone else.

### You Are Important

No one else can express this power as you do. It is important that you embrace this idea on a daily basis.

*I am the Power and Presence of the One Thinker, and I align myself with this Power Right Now! I do the work. I accept my good. I acknowledge and receive all of the blessings the Universe has to offer me right now.*

### The Power Behind Your Expertise

When we live from a place of knowing consciously that we are aligned with and tapped into an infinite wellspring of thought, which co-generates with The Divine, we sense this Power is, in fact, doing the work by means of you and me.

When I was an apprentice carpenter, I had a boss who was up my ass all day long. I was 20 years old and probably needed close supervision, but the result was that I couldn't scratch my nose without eliciting some criticism. One day, a neighbor stopped by and asked if I could do a small project on her home. Always being short on cash, I said yes, in spite of my lack of confidence in my skills at the time. I discovered that without my boss riding me, I could figure out all kinds of things for myself. I learned I could work in a self-directed way, completely autonomously. As it happened, the side work, which I was kind of scared of doing on my own, also made me a much better employee.

This is not to say mistakes aren't still made, but with a commitment to do better every day, a mistake becomes a teaching moment. Remember the difference between a good carpenter and a poor one—the good one knows how to fix his mistakes. Teaching moments applied to life are a changed life.

This is important to know in a few ways. The biggest idea is to work toward removing dependency from our working relationships. Even with our boss. This doesn't mean we can't or shouldn't take direction, but rather that we are committed to being a co-creator in the relationship. We partner with all of life.

Another way this is important is to understand we always know more than we think we do.

And lastly, our connection with creativity provides solutions to most problems that present themselves throughout a given day.

Instead of being overly dependent on the boss, unless I was given direction in a specific way to address a specific task, I learned it was far more important for me to have a plan of my own and run that plan by the boss. This is just as important for the new guy as it is for the experienced, 5-year journeyman. Of course, some bosses are control freaks, or may need for you to prove you know what you're doing before you're given the flexibility of self-direction. Even in such a case, it's really all about a way of thinking, regardless of how the boss sees it.

## The Rabbit and the Hat

When you use the power of thought, miraculous things happen. As all thought is creative, it sometimes feels as if thought is magical, like you've pulled a rabbit out of a hat.

Creativity has no limits.

*That is, unless you're a carpenter trying to write a book!*

In all seriousness, try as you may, you can never run out of creative ideas. Its playground is an infinite field of possibilities and outcomes. Remember Einstein's quote, *"Imagination is more important than knowledge"*? Our imagination is a dance between the conscious and unconscious mind. All we have ever thought, or are thinking currently, or will think about in the future, makes up our consciousness. Your life, my life, all our lives are demonstrations of this consciousness, as individuals AND collectively.

## Thought Appears to Be Magical

I remember like it was yesterday how I first experienced that intuitive voice I spoke of earlier. The quiet voice guiding me to the successful completion of the project. In time, at 20 years old, I became the de facto leader of the crew I was working with because of it.

We were supposed to be building a deck. Our overly directive boss was gone, and we had run out of work to do. To move forward in building our project, we needed to place a concrete pier pad to hold a post and beam, to build the deck with. A fairly simple thing to do. Our boss had not instructed us to do this. My workmates, two men who were both ten years older than I, were hesitant to move forward, afraid of making a mistake. We had not been directed to build the deck, but it was the next obvious task, as all the materials were on site. Besides, our boss could be a real prick about having guys stand around on the clock!

The other guys were not showing initiative, so I grabbed a couple of anchor nuts used for bolting down a foundation plate, tied them on the end of 20 feet of string and said, "Why not just hang this string down from the end of the beam, and that will tell us where to place the concrete pier?"

My workmates, who had seniority in the company over me, revealed their fears: "Well, I don't know," "What if it's wrong?" "Ed will get mad."

When Ed returned, he was mad all right! Mad to see his three-man crew sitting on their asses! Mind you, I had set the string line (which I later learned was called a plumb bob), and had everything in place to move forward. The other two guys were going to be looking for other work in a couple of weeks anyway, so they had nothing to gain by employing initiative.

The intuitive voice I experienced that day has served me well over the years—whenever I honor it, of course, which, sad to say, I have not always done. But now that I know better, I try to honor it as soon as I am aware of its message. In this way, I can confidently start my day with the affirmation, "Everything is always working out for me!" And mean it!

## The Field of Infinite Possibilities

This experience happened to me as a young apprentice, but clearly, it's been an important lesson for me in a couple of ways.

Looking back—though I would not have had the language to express what I was experiencing until much later—there was a method of figuring stuff out I wasn't even aware I was using. At the same time, I did have a sense I was tapping into some kind of cosmic database. To have an intuitive sense of how to build things should not have come so naturally, because I didn't grow up around guys building stuff; I grew up on an isolated Air Force Base where nothing was built or remodeled. I seemed to have an intuitive connection to a trade I would later come to see as a calling. As a result, I have spoken to scores of men and women about feeling "called" to work. There is just something soulful in that experience.

The great teacher Allan Watts once said, *"If you do what you love, you'll never have to work a day in your life."* This has been absolutely true for me even after 30-plus years of crawling, lifting, climbing, and head scratching my way through building things.

I feel fortunate in this calling. I did not get rich, but I was self-supporting through my own contributions. And better yet, I helped to support a couple of families, at least for as long as I was officially a part of them, and then some.

It was also in this trade work where I would discover and learn to understand how to access and use a power greater than myself that was not bound by anything except my own limited thinking. I came to find a God that works, and works flawlessly, when I allow this Force and Source to do its thing by means of my life.

I came to see that God Consciousness is as good a word for me to use to describe my discovery as any. God expressing Itself as Consciousness through all of Life as the thing It thinks about, bound only by the Nature of Its own Being—which is infinite!

## Life Is Consciousness

I would have this experience of tapping into this inner problem-solver thousands of times throughout the course of my career as a carpenter/contractor. With an inward smile to myself, I would come to think of it as the mind of Jesus coaching me up. After all, we were in the same trade union. Years later, I would be exposed to the writings of Rev. Emmet Fox, and he would call this Christ Consciousness.

I find it serendipitous that the thinking of a carpenter two thousand years ago was nudging me along to find solutions in my own carpentry work at the time. Turns out, there is a passage from Paul of Tarsus, which speaks to the idea that "we have the mind of the Christ." `

Staying on this biblical track for a moment, Paul also said not to be conformed to the world, but instead to be transformed by the renewal of your mind, to test out what the will of God is for you, to discern "what is good, acceptable, and perfect."

Now I admit, I'm not a biblical scholar, but I did take to these passages when I came upon them as an adult. They have tremendous power in them to this day. We need to have the courage to explore this power in a new way, beyond our current thinking, and make ourselves open to finding ways to consciously include these ideas in our daily lives. When we do, we shall find a hidden power for all of our seeming problems of the day.

# What's in Your Chapter 4 Toolbox?

In speaking to the challenges of daily living in the first three chapters, we began to explore the possibility of a Higher Power that assists you in your commitment to shift and lift the tendency of thought from what you do NOT want to what you DO want. In Chapter 4, we began to evolve our tools from offering a psychological self-help solution to offering a spiritually empowered solution to be demonstrated!

So now, get your pencil and your thinking power ready, knowing each prompt below may require a moment of quiet and reflection, in order for you to receive your answers.

1.  In considering your life over the past several days, list six things in your life you found challenging, annoying, or which just really pissed you off; they can be large or small.

_____

_____

_____

_____

2.  Next, in considering your life over the past several days, list six things you would label as good—large or small.

_____

_____

_____

_____

3.  In considering your "good things great and small," imagine each item on your list as a gift sent special delivery, directly to you, as if from a Cosmic Amazon deliveryman. Do you feel any deeper sense of appreciating? If so, how exactly?

_____

_____

_____

_____

_____

_____

4.   From the perspective of appreciating the Cosmic Amazon delivery person filling your "thought order," how does your interpretation of your list of aggravations in Prompt #1 change?

_____

_____

_____

_____

5.   Try working with the affirmation below for a week, in earnest, paying particular attention to whether your week on balance was easier, harder, or if it experienced no shift at all.

> _I am the Power and Presence of the One Thinker, and I align myself with this Power Right Now! I do the work. I accept my good. I acknowledge and receive all of the blessings the Universe has to offer me right now. I am grateful for all that Life affords me!_

6.   After the experiment is finished, journal any thoughts you have on what you experienced.

_____

_____

_____

_____

_____

_____

_____

_____

_____

(There's more space at the back of the book for further journaling, as needed.)

# Chapter 5
# This Power Is Free

Isn't it good to know this Power we've been defining is free? And it's inexhaustible! We can play with it in any way we desire. We can't waste it, for there is plenty. It is our Inexhaustible Natural Resource! So, why not experiment with it? The only requirement for using it is to use it! You and I are the point of power in which this resource is applied. This Power is Infinite in nature and can only be used through our life, as the activity of our thought—for *Thought as Life* is its very Nature.

Considering this carefully, we see how important it is to be mindful of what we're thinking. It's not just what we think about; it's *how* we think about it. Not only in the ways we're consciously thinking about our challenges, but also the ways our unconscious is shaping thought. How can we know the stuff we aren't consciously thinking about? What evidence is there of the interplay between our conscious desires and the unconscious thoughts that lie beneath them? We need only look around us and give witness to the life we are currently living. Is this life my best life now?

Is it not self-evident we would not consciously set out to sabotage ourselves and the life we live? If there is struggle or lack and limitation standing in our way, it's because there are levels of thought operating in an unconscious way that must be shifted in order for our thinking to serve us better.

*What about race, social standing, education, discrimination? Don't these have an impact on my life, as well?* The short answer is yes.

Obviously, there are ways we think collectively that can have serious impact on the way folks experience life as individuals. Just like the man who is clueless about what he's thinking, or the way he says what he's thinking, society can be just as unconsciously clueless, hateful, and cruel. This cluelessness demonstrates itself in society as racism, sexism, and discrimination in all kinds of ways. Unfortunately, we have been locked into these systems for so long they have become normalized. Complicating matters is that many white people today do not feel like the dominant group any longer. People everywhere are working harder than ever and struggling to stay ahead.

That folks are working their asses off to get what they need does not change the fact that if you are a person of color in 2020, you still have to deal with challenges that white folk do not have to contend with. I cannot see how any church, any government system, or even electing a Black man president can eliminate this scourge unless all of us involved own those parts within our thinking that contribute to these longtime problems. When we as individuals come to see that to change our thinking is to change our life, WE TOGETHER change the lives of those around us as well. In this way, your life matters, Black Lives Matter, Gay Lives Matter, and on and on, so that in the end, ultimately, GRAY-MATTER MATTERS! All of us thinking collectively to create a world that works for everyone!

## We Got the Power!

Yes, we got the Power! We use it all the time in ways conscious and unconscious. It beats our hearts. It is breathing us. We are breathing it! It is every thought we are aware of, and how we do it. Scientists tell us the average person thinks 60,000 thoughts a day, and 85% of those are the same thoughts as yesterday. Thus, the importance of monitoring the tendency of our thinking becomes paramount! This means we're often caught in a web of our own making, ensnared by yesterday's losses, or dreaming, scheming, or fearing tomorrow. In this way, then, our point of Power is Right Now—and IS our point of Power!

This power of thought is undeniable; it's been THE theme throughout this book. Let me now say to you, there is a Power behind the thought, a transcendent Power, a Cosmic Intelligence. This is not a new discovery of modern man, and in fact, one could say the ancients may have been more in touch with this Power in their own way. In their understanding, this Power was often parental, something to be feared and sacrificed to. In one version, a story similar to other ancient stories, the Son of God Himself was sacrificed to make things right between us and the One God. What you and I do with this information is up to us.

What I want to point to here is how the Carpenter spoke of the Great Comforter, The Great Counselor, another name for Holy Spirit. He spoke of the Father as the Aramaic *Abba*, which translates much closer to the modern word, "Daddy" implying a much sweeter and more intimate relationship with the Divine— certainly within the Jewish understanding of such things at the time.

The man Jesus taught successful strategies for growing in ways close and intimate with Spirit, *and* from the practicalities of making our way through life. This aspect of his teachings has been given a back seat to concerns over eternal damnation, and frankly a base human need for certainty and blame. For those faiths living within a construct of conformity, there can be tremendous comfort; but within those faiths there generally isn't a therapeutic modality available for dealing with what drives these behaviors they find so sinful, except for a reinforcement of the idea that the sinner is unworthy because he exists in a state of sin. There IS a forgiveness-of-sin promise, which may or may not deal with deeper underlying struggles. And so, while forgiveness is important, what's just as crucial for any spiritual evolution is a healing and transformational construct.

Within this system, when one strays at the leadership level, the leaders say, "hate the sin, not the sinner." It is a kind of spiritual bypass where public penance may or may not be demonstrated, and the carnage left in their wake causes irreparable harm to the lives affected by someone's poor judgment at best, egregious behavior, arrogance, or hubris, at worst.

The net effect is for folks to become disenchanted with religion and to want to pitch the whole proposition of *God* altogether. As it is, it's not that difficult for people to take their Sundays back. Besides, the idea that "Jesus saves" only works if you feel saved.

This is why I've used the subtitle, *Finding a God that Works*. Spirituality is like a diet; it really doesn't work unless you find one you can live with. And by living with it, I mean sticking with it.

We can start with the idea I learned long ago from the writer Ernest Holmes, when he said, *"There is a Power for Good in the Universe, available to everyone, and you can Use It!"*

Call the Power what you will. We have certainly explored many names so far in this book. What's in a name anyway? *God* is an English derivative of the Anglo-Saxon *Got*. And *Got* is a German translation from the Greek *Theos*. Early Greek translators of Jesus' writings knew at least some Aramaic, the language of Jesus, though Aramaic manuscripts have not been available ever— only surmised to exist. The word for God in Aramaic is Alaha/Alaho, which was translated into Greek texts as Abba (not the pop music group!). The Hebrew was YHWH; Hebrews did not pronounce the name of God, but according to text, that's the name Moses came down the mountain with, hence the name Yahweh. Obviously translation can be tricky business. So you can see, even at the most basic understandings of the Divine, God is far more than we think It is!

*"A rose by any other name would smell as sweet."*

Consider that this Power is not bound by time or space. It is a reflection of Infinite Intelligence, an Infinite Heart, the wellspring of All this is Good. There is a Pattern of Perfection throughout this manifest Life, which is an emanation of Spirit Itself. It is present in every aspect of material and non-material existence, in ways seen and unseen. It is within you, within me, within all things.

We got the Power! It's now up to us to use It!

## Same Ol', Same Ol'

I've heard it said, "Some people live a single year for their entire lifetime, while others live a lifetime in every single year." By now you may be imagining ways in which your life could be different by using the power of thought in a conscious way. Living consciously does not mean we are eliminating the hardships of life; we are simply using hardship to create a new idea for life. In this way, we use hardship as a tool for transformation. We then no longer live the same day over and over again in a cycle of futility and struggle. Instead, we are set free to live creatively.

By inviting the Infinite Power of Divine Intelligence to make Itself known through and as our life, we intuitively draw to us new and dynamic ideas that offer solutions to problems, which up until now may have had us stymied or confused. When we allow the Infinite Source of Love to crack us open, we find a Deep Wellspring of Love, Compassion, and Empathy within us, awaiting our activation of It. We understand Cosmic Intelligence is not bound by anything that came before. We can confidently know we not only capture those ideas, but there is an Infinite Power backing our play, from which we can draw an inner strength. Infinite Power. That's a lot!

Stop for a moment, and take a breath right now.

*In this moment, as I take a breath, I realize I am breathing in the very Breath of Life Itself. I feel a sense of restoration and vitality. I remember that I am an expression of the Living Spirit. Spirit and I are One. From this place of conscious unity with the One, I now open my mind to new and creative ideas. I let my mind flow until it lights upon that New Thought, which lifts me out of any sense of confusion and into clarity of thought. I allow clarity to be the rule of my life. My thought is clear; the crooked way has been made straight.*

70

*Taking another breath, I release this breath with a sense of gratitude and confidence, knowing I am on the right path. I now let it be so.*

No more "Same 'ol, Same 'ol," but rather a life that has been transformed by the renewing of the mind.

### Shift and Lift!

What's important to know here is we are shifting the *tendency* of our thoughts from ways of thinking that no longer serve us, to ways of thinking that support our highest good. Don't be surprised if this is difficult to do consistently. If it were easy to do we'd have done it already! Sometimes, this old thinking is so HEAVY. Thoughts of fear, despair, catastrophe, and personal safety are all emotionally dense and burdensome. The only way to heal them is to acknowledge and release them!

We all have examples in the physical world of how we've lifted heavy objects like couches, refrigerators, pianos, and even cars! How do we lift such things? Leverage. By finding the right tool, say a crow bar, we *shift* the object just enough to *lift* it. We get that leverage point again. We shift it again, just enough to lift it again, until, in time, we have that piano right where we want it! Or at least close enough.

We can shift and lift our thinking world in just the same way. We are so busy trying to shoo away errant thoughts of despair, of longing, of self-recrimination and the fear of taking risks, when we should be shifting and lifting our attention to ways of thinking that are more uplifting and affirmative. Meaning, we focus on what we DO want rather than what we DON'T want. Little lifts at a time, little shifts at a time. And the leverage point? Spiritual Power! Spiritual Power is the Lever. Our desire is the fulcrum. Our thought gives direction.

Try it now, taking a breath, feeling refreshment and the presence of this moment (the Lever).

*I am living in the flow of love. I attract and maintain healthy friendships where I feel supported and connected.* (The Shift)

*I know and accept myself as an emanation of the Cosmic Thinker, knowing every day, in every way, I am making choices for my highest good.* (The Lift!)

Think of a particularly difficult area in your life. See if you can write an affirmation around it that is more uplifting than your current thinking. Try it!

You got this!

### Do It Now!

If you're not used to living consciously and you're still with me here, chances are what I am sharing with you may be resonating within your thinking. I'm grateful you're still here, but what's really important is that at some point, you have to put the book down and put these ideas into practice. Hopefully you've taken some time to use the tools at the end of these chapters? If not, this would be a great time to do it.

Do it now.

Identify what you don't want. Claim what you DO want. Know there is a Power greater than you are, and it is backing your play.

When used in a conscious way, this Spiritual Power helps focus the tendency of our attention upon the new thought we have for ourselves and our greater life. We are growing. We are awake, aware, and alive. We understand all is Divine Thought in expression, and we are one with this Cosmic Thought. We turn away from our old way of seeing the world and our place in it, and instead confidently know we are being shifted and lifted into a new way of being. We have been reborn into an awareness of the Oneness of Life, and it is good! It is done! It is the Eternal Now expressing IN you, THROUGH you, and AS you!

## The Only Cost

There is a Power for Good in the Universe available to everyone, and we can use It. The only cost involved is the effort it takes to *remember to use It*, and to use It in real time, in a conscious way. Sometimes, even when we know better, we'll be like that ol' rodeo cowboy trying to wrestle the steer of the world of conditions one more time. Hopefully, we remember to let go and let God *before* we get the horn!

Of course, the "steer" and the struggle we have with it are both thought forms of our own making, usually manipulative schemes that have more concerns of the ego, with little room for Spirit. When we use the power of our thought coupled with divine wisdom in a conscious way, for ourselves and for others, we are powerful beyond measure. With Spirit, we can build even better companies and the best of relationships. We heal the sick and even heal our sickly finances.

### Do It Like Nike!

Like the Nike ads say, just do it! Do it in your own way, but do it! You cannot do it wrong unless you don't use it at all!

I've been speaking to the power of thought, or what the ancients have called the power of prayer. You, however, need to think of it in whatever way aligns with your understanding. Again, this is what the tools at the end of each chapter are for. It doesn't matter what I say, what your spouse says, what any well-meaning friends have to say, or even what your local pastor thinks. What is important is what you think. And not some downloaded Internet BS opinion of what you *should* think. What do *you* think? How do you think? And is there room in your thinking to find a new way of connecting deeper to and with the Divine? What is the Divine to you? Who is the Divine to you? Open your mind, and more importantly, open your heart to the Divine Song longing to be heard by the ear of your own heart.

Maybe say something like this:

*As I breathe in this Breath of Life, I am now open and receptive to a deeper experience of the Divine expressing in, through, and as my life. I am open to the Infinite Heart of the Divine Itself, which now lifts my heart and raises my thinking that I might better demonstrate the Infinite*

*Power of the Living Spirit, as my life, which is rich, full, and abundant. It is abundant in love, connection, financial prosperity, and creative ideas that raise my life and the lives of others. In confidence and gratitude, I release my life as the divine unfoldment expressing as me.*

And so it is!

Just do it!

*Just did!*

### The Coin of the Realm

Attention and intention are two very powerful practices in this New Order of thought. Intention is the mental activity of focusing the mind in a chosen direction; intentions are actually the easiest part of this exercise. But as we've all heard before, the road to Hell is paved with good...what? Yes, intentions. So, it's not enough to simply have intention, unless we can harness the attention to see things through. Intention points to light. Attention is what happens when we see the light.

Attention is where the power of the heart brings emotion and feeling to that thought (intention) to help anchor our focus until the task at hand is accomplished. Think about an interest you're really passionate and enthusiastic about; does it not naturally and easily get more of your attention? Not only does it get more of your attention, but also when engaged with that interest, time seems to stand still.

If you're a person like me with "wandering interests," (can we call it creative?) this can be challenging. We may have to find ways to get our attention snagged and then keep it hooked long enough to complete a given task (as in, how do we move a big ol' pile of dirt? One shovel load at a time).

This is why back in the Chapter 2 toolbox, on pg. 33, I asked you to name three projects you'd love to do if you knew you had all the time and money to carry it through. By asking you to answer that prompt *without* the usual qualifiers as to why it can or cannot be done, what you're really doing is inviting the heart to have a say, without asking it directly. Because what if I'd asked you to list three projects that make your heart sing? You'd roll your eyeballs and toss the book away.

But HEART is what I'm talking about.

Whether IN-tention or AT-tention, with either one, emotion can be a strong ally. Of course, not all emotions are created equal. Strong feelings of despair keep us weighed down in inaction. And on the other end of the spectrum, manic joy may burn us out before we even get started. To use emotion as an ally, consider ones that could be the most helpful in their application.

I just looked up synonyms for joy: Elation. Delight. Merriment. Playfulness.

These are just a few that appeal to me. I invite any emotion that helps sustain my enthusiastic attention to a given task. If it has joy in it, I find I can stick with it better and stay motivated.

There's another strong emotion that can help us stay motivated as well, but we want to be careful with this one. That emotion is anger. Now, I'm not saying anger is bad, per se, but we must be mindful with it. Anger has, history shows, been a catalyst for change, and in this way harnessed anger can be used to get folks to stop talking and start acting.

Anger when misused, on the other hand, can cause serious collateral damage. Think of the spouse who waits to be angry before speaking up about an issue, or the employee who gets so angry he quits his job over a communication breakdown. It is never helpful to stuff down resentments until they boil over in a fit of rage. When trying to communicate legitimate concerns while angry and raging, all anyone hears is the anger. In this way, it is not effective, even with legitimate concerns.

As St. Paul said, "be angry and not sin." Be angry and avoid error, error in thought, error in speech, error in actions. The Civil Rights actions of Dr. King illustrate this beautifully. Be angry and not sin. Be angry and practice non-violence. Dr. Martin Luther King was truly masterful at this, because he was passionate—yes!

Even more to the point, he practiced non-violence in his words as well as his actions.

But that's a whole 'nother subject! Read Marshall Rosenberg's book, *Nonviolent Communication*, on this one. I'm still working on it!

For now, let's simply remember that intention and attention are the coin of the realm. These two aspects of thought become super powers when combined with enthusiasm and joy. With them, we can heal any situation or challenge that life may present to us. And that's a good thing!

*As I take in a deep breath, I allow myself to surrender to this present moment. All cares and concerns for the day slide away as I claim this moment as my own. In this moment, I consider ways to allow joy into my life. I consider the experiences of the joyful expressions I embrace: Having a moment with my beloved, the exuberance of perfect weather, the release in sharing a joke with a friend.*

*Knowing joy is an expression of the Living Spirit, I open myself to joy right now. I feel a sense that all is well, that all my needs are met and then some. I experience love as friendship. I sense my connection to the larger world. I am moved by compassion and empathy to do what is mine to do, and leave the rest to Divine Unfoldment.*

*I now step confidently and joyfully with gratitude into this day, knowing the Spirit of the Lord is upon me!*

And so it is!

### A New Understanding of Life

When we have an understanding of life as an Infinite Flow of Good available to everyone, and we can use it, it naturally sets up an expectation of good that may or may not be evident. Sometimes we look around, and there is no seeming evidence of our shifted consciousness—good or bad. In fact, sometimes it gets worse before it gets better. This can be discouraging, to be sure, but this is actually good news because the struggle is pointing the way to the solution.

I remember years ago when I started experimenting with this New Thought stuff. I started my day with quiet time. I was carving out time in my hectic day for spiritual study. I was working with consciousness in prayer and meditation. My personal life was not great but doing okay. On the business side, however, things were turning to crap. It seemed everywhere I turned I had labor challenges, slow paying customers, and I was having to bid rather than negotiate my new contracts. It was a slog! I was sharing with my friend Nancy about how difficult it all was, and gave her the whole "ain't it awful" story, and how my consciousness was not strong enough to demonstrate the profitable business I was visioning for myself.

Nancy said, "Mike, there ain't nothin' wrong with your consciousness. Look at all this 'struggle' you've demonstrated for yourself. Seems to me you have a mighty consciousness—for demonstrating what you DON'T want. We just need to shift your focus on the good, and to know this Reality of Good is yours NOW!"

I did not want to hear that—let alone believe it!

So, I asked somebody else, whom I knew was working with the power of thought, and gave them my story, and they said the same damn thing! Double Crap!

So, my friend Maureen said to me, "You mean to tell me no one is calling you to bid work?"

"Well, yes, the phone's been ringing, but only for these little dingbat home repair jobs!"

I SO dislike handyman work!

"Mike," says Maureen, "you are to say yes to the next job that comes in, no matter how small."

Says I, "You don't understand, Maureen! It takes just as much time to set up one of these small jobs as a large one. I want the big jobs. I'm a well-established contractor. This work is beneath me!"

"Nevertheless," (yes, she does talk this way!) "Nevertheless, you are to take the next job that comes your way. Bid it properly, the way you would any other job. But take the job. You need to understand you are turning your Good away. When you're doing mental work, and inviting the Divine to work with you (in other words, *praying*), and turning away work, you are saying NO to the Universe. Stop doing that. You ARE demonstrating; you're just not seeing it! Say YES to the next job."

I reluctantly agreed to do so, and I continued to do my spiritual work, and I bid these smaller jobs, but with a shifted consciousness of YES around all of it.

Within a week, I was working on a building doing handyman tasks I hated. Ironically, that job ended up leading to the largest job and best year I'd had in contracting up until that point.

Spirit has a plan that is within my own plan, but I have to make room for it. I must not only invite the Infinite Power in to play, but I must then allow for Its demonstration to make Itself known—by means of my life, my business, my relationships, and especially my creative endeavors!

Spirit responds to our thought. This is, after all, what any prayer is. In this way, Spirit takes direction. In fact, Spirit knows only to say *Yes*. This is why we must be careful of what we speak, to be mindful of how we speak about ourselves and our interests throughout all of life. Spirit knows only to say *Yes* because It is Love expressing in, through, and as All. A perfect, unconditional Love, bound only by the Nature of Its own Being, which is Infinite! Motivated by its Infinite impulse for Creative Expression and bound only by our belief in It.

For God so loved the world that It has created *you* in Its image and likeness, that It may create and experience more of Life, by means of you, and everyone else too! Spirit is the Light unto the world. And so are you!

With careful consideration, you will find that the light that extinguishes the darkness around any errant thought is the Light of Love expressing. When the Ancient proclaimed, "God is Love," it was not only a proclamation of truth; it was pointing the way to the very resource from which to think. We have a new understanding of life. We are a Point of Power through which the Life of God expresses as all of Life. Yours AND mine. And when we use it consciously together, we can transform the planet for the Good of ALL!

## The Thrill of Victory!

For me, there is no bigger thrill than witnessing the power of focused thought in all its demonstrations! This is true in demonstrating for myself, and even more so to witness it in others. It is thrilling to bear witness to the demonstration of consciousness in expression. It underscores our faith, confidence, and even our courage to use The Power in all of our daily concerns, in ever expanding ways.

In my building days, I felt tremendous satisfaction watching a building go up from concept to plan, plan to dirt, dirt to finish. I have come to see that life works in much the same way. The use of consciousness provides the vehicle for demonstrating profitable businesses, which serve the customer, the business owner, and all of the people involved in the enterprise. And I have proven it time and again in my construction business. As a result, I've enjoyed the fruits of profitability as well as experiencing that sweet spot of life with its joy, happiness, and prosperity propagated by the seed of conscious thought.

Even more importantly, I have become a far more awakened version of my former self, and I am gratefully delivered from my old mindset.

Don't take my word for it. Experiment with these ideas yourself. Play with this Power of Thought. Develop a way of seeing beyond simple appearances, and allow for a greater truth to come forth.

Here's what I know. God always works, and God is always there. And so, this book isn't really about finding *A* God. It is about allowing God. And considering where an old redneck like my recovering self has come from, that part right there is a pretty successful life-shifting and life-lifting retrofit.

We're now at the end of this little book, and there have been many questions thrown at you, which only you can answer. So, if you're ready to rebuild something with a solid foundation that ensures stability and reliability, if you're convinced the old bones and old ways of thinking are no longer sufficient to keep your house standing, if you have found there is greater, stronger, and more powerful in store for you—then claim your right to the Good that's available now. Give witness to the Power in your Life. Acknowledge it! Celebrate it!

So, let's grab that toolbox, and like Larry the Cable Guy before us ... let's git 'er done!

# Epilogue

You would think a guy who's had your attention for nearly a hundred pages would be spent and have nothing left to say. Yeah, that's what I thought too.

Then all Hell broke loose.

By all accounts we're in the middle of the Covid-19 pandemic. At the time of writing this epilogue (June 2020), it looks like we're going to have to ride this out for another ten months. So far, 110,000 people have died, and by the time you read this that number will likely have grown. People have been "safe at home" for three months now. It threatens to set us back on a slow growth recovery arc that could take a decade to dig out from, even as some are telling us it's going to be fine and it's time to get back to work. And still, we're in for ten more months of precautions for a foe we cannot see and whose presence makes itself known only when someone is sick, possibly infecting scores of others in its wake.

The disparity of the haves and have-nots has rarely been so visibly demonstrated. As workers, whom few people give notice to, put themselves and their families at risk of infection, stockholders of All Things Internet are reaping a bonanza. For the fortunate few who have retirement savings, the major stockholders of corporations and their leadership have, for fifty years now, been slyly paying us off through our 401K's with pennies as they skim off millions, setting working people against each other while they laugh all the way to the bank. What's to be done?

Within weeks of being stuck at home, millions of us witnessed on television and social media the killing of George Floyd as he was in the custody of the Minneapolis Police Dept. Filmed for all to see, the arresting officer, looking dead-on into the camera in the most careless and calloused way, free of concern or consequence, held his knee on the neck of George Floyd for close to nine minutes, as Floyd died weeping for his mother, "I can't breathe."

People have been taking to the streets ever since. Black Lives Matter may currently be the rallying cry against police brutality, but this has been a call for EVERYONE to wake up, take responsibility for what is ours to do, and take action to make things right, once and for all. After a sketchy start, people are taking it to the streets, not to destroy, but to rebuild.

Does this have a familiar ring to it? Waking up and taking responsibility have been the common themes of this book. Yet to "find a God that works," only to hide from the troubles of the world or to feel impotent in the face of world conditions, is simply not going to cut it. You must allow your social conscience some consideration as well.

I urge you to open your mind and your heart, because whether you are liberal or conservative, wrong is wrong.

Killing is wrong, and making a killing over making a profit is wrong. Both are immoral—God or no god.

Now, there is nothing wrong with free enterprise, and I'm pretty sure you've surmised from the tone of this book that I am a free-market guy. Capitalism is a great innovator. The system, however, is riddled with inequity. Corporate interests are getting away with abusive monopolies and gigantic tax loopholes because they have convinced the Chambers of Commerce that we're all in this together. But there is a big difference between the small business owner who puts it all on the line every day and the corporate leader who has no skin in the game—except *maybe* his reputation. The corporation is treated by the law as an individual, which, by default, makes it an infinite entity. Any sole proprietor competing against a corporate franchise has little chance of doing better than making a living, because most franchises are simply schemes for the investment bankers and their investors to skim for control and fees.

Now put capitalism and racism together. They *are* tied to one another through slavery. What's happening on our streets can only be addressed with a strong commitment to lasting change, yet the economic system we're operating under is geared more towards Wall Street than Main Street. Both streets lead to ruin for everyone if we do not address the racial and economic inequity once and for all.

We can start by speaking up for our brothers and sisters of color. Perhaps the step before that is to *see* them as brothers and sisters; people we sometimes disagree with, but love just the same, where our blood of togetherness is not only thicker than water, it is thicker than profit too.

It is time to stop worshipping the pursuers of wealth as High Priests who have all the answers.

It is time to call out the false narrative of how we are broke because we should've gone to school or don't work hard enough. *The system* is broken! It is broken because those at the top skim off 90% of the milk—and all of the cream—then have the gall to lecture the rest of us on being immoral or lazy. Corporate institutions break their new toy then fix the blame on anyone else, and expect everyone else to pay for it. It's the *Invisible Hand of the Market* for all but themselves.

So, while I've just been espousing for close to a hundred pages that there is a Power for Good in the Universe, available to everyone, in these upheaved times you and I are going to have to step up and BE the Agents for this Power to assert Itself in the Human realm.

The sad fact is, the starting line for economic opportunity favors some more than others; the wrong race and gender is a deficit for all. The Infinite Spirit within Its Cosmic Process created the human race, and humans created racism (Jane Elliot). This means WE—you and I— must address it and make it right.

We have knowingly or unknowingly created Capitalism. God did not bestow it from on high. And this means it can be fixed.

Take the best parts, an efficient engine for innovation, creativity, and profitability for the most people possible—including the people doing the work! That's doable. But WE have to insist that it be made so. As Teresa of Avila once said, "Yours are the hands through which He blesses all the world."

So, this is a tall order for all of us. And…you cannot give away something you haven't got! Work daily knowing there is that within you which has all Power, Knowledge, Love and Creativity. Put it to work for you and yours, and community. Raise those around you in prayer, in opportunity, with respect and love.

And with the ballot box!

It's time for you to be the change!

# RESOURCES

**BLOGS**

- NewThoughtEvolutionary.Wordpress.com (Dr. Jim Lockard)
- CSLGH.com/presidents-blog/ @ cslgh.org
- BlueCollarSpirituality-blog-blog.tumblr.com/

**BOOKS**

- Michael Bernard Beckwith, *Spiritual Liberation*
- Michael Bernard Beckwith, *40 Day Mind Fast, Soul Feast*
- Brené Brown, *Daring Greatly*
- Carolyn Jane Bohler, *God the What? What Our Metaphors for God Reveal about Our Beliefs in God*
- Eric Butterworth, *Spiritual Economics: The Principles and Process of True Prosperity*
- Eric Butterworth, *The Universe Is Calling: Opening to the Divine Through Prayer*
- Stephen Cope, *The Great Work of Your Life*
- Emmet Fox, *Sermon on the Mount*
- Patrick Harbula, *Meditation (A Start Here Guide)*
- Ernest Holmes, *Creative Mind and Success*
- Ernest Holmes, *Living the Science of Mind*
- Ernest Holmes, *The Science of Mind*
- Ernest Holmes, *This Thing Called You*
- Theresa McMorrow Jordan, *Get Crowned*
- George M. Lamsa, *The Holy Bible from the Ancient Eastern Text: George M. Lamsa's Translations from the Aramaic of the Peshitta*

- Dr. Jim Lockard, *Sacred Thinking*
- Mary Manin Morrissey, *Building your Field of Dreams*
- Maria Nemeth, *The Energy of Money: A Spiritual Guide to Financial and Personal Fulfillment*
- Fr. Richard Rohr, *The Universal Christ: How a Forgotten Reality Can Change Everything We See, Hope for, and Believe*
- Huston Smith, *The World's Religions*
- Edward Viljoen, *The Bhagavad Gita: The Song of God Retold in Simplified English*
- Bill W., *Alcoholics Anonymous*
- Angela Carole Brown, writer/editor, graphic artist, musician www.angelacarolebrown.com

## PODCASTS

- Alan Watts Podcast
- On Being with Krista Tippet
- The Tim Ferris Show
- The Good One, Vulture
- World Spirituality, Rev. Paul John Roach, Stitcher
- Unity Online Radio, Stitcher

## LOOKING FOR OTHERS WHO THINK THIS WAY?

- Google "Centers for Spiritual Living near me"
- Center for Spiritual Living Granada Hills @ www.cslgh.org
- Unity Worldwide Ministries
- Agape International Spiritual Center
- Michael McMorrow @ revmike@cslgh.org

# Notes — Thoughts — Tools

Made in the USA
Columbia, SC
21 December 2021

51945682R00065